Contents

About
Vocabulary Centers
Grades 3-4

What's Great About This Book

Centers are a wonderful, fun way for students to practice important skills. The 12 centers in this book are self-contained and portable. Students may work at a desk, at a table, or even on the floor. Once you've made the centers, they're ready to use any time.

What's in This Book

| **Teacher and student directions** include how to make and use the center | **Full-color task cards and games** | **Reproducible activity sheets** to practice vocabulary skills | **Self-checking answer keys** |

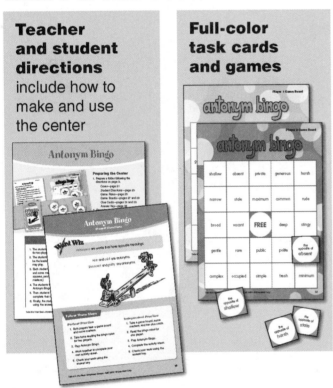

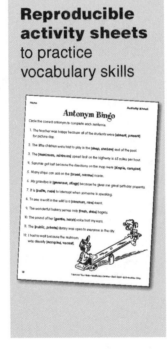

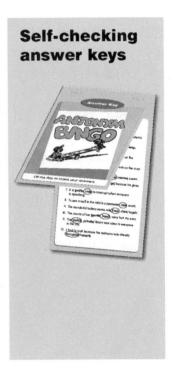

How to Use the Centers

The centers are intended for skill practice, not to introduce skills. It is important to model the use of each center before students do the task independently.

Questions to Consider:

- Will students select a center, or will you assign the centers?
- Will there be a specific block of time for centers, or will the centers be used throughout the day?
- Where will you place the centers for easy access by students?
- What procedure will students use when they need help with the center tasks?
- How will you track the tasks and centers completed by each student?

Making a File Folder Center

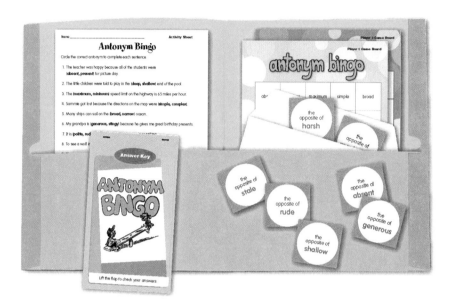

Folder centers are easily stored in a box or file crate. Students take a folder to their desks to complete the task.

Materials:

- folder with pockets
- envelopes
- marking pens and pencils
- scissors
- stapler
- glue or two-sided tape
- small objects for markers (e.g., dried beans, pennies, etc.)

Folder Back

Folder Front

Steps to Follow:

1. Laminate the cover. Tape it to the front of the folder.

2. Laminate the student directions page. Tape it to the back of the folder.

3. Laminate the self-checking answer key for each center. Cut the page in half. Staple the cover on top of the answer key. Place the answer key in the left-hand pocket.

4. Place activity sheets and any other supplies in the left-hand pocket.

5. Laminate the task cards and puzzle pieces. Place each set in a labeled envelope in the right-hand pocket.

6. If needed for a center, laminate the sorting mat or game board and place it in the right-hand pocket of the folder.

Center Checklist

Student Names

Centers

Centers											
Fabulous Synonyms											
Antonym Bingo											
Homophone Match											
Prefix Preview											
Working Suffixes											
Animal Analogies											
Geography Compound Words											
Funny Nouns											
Wild Weather Tic-Tac-Toe											
Playing with Polygons											
Borrowed Words											
Multiple Meanings											

Fabulous Synonyms

Preparing the Center

1. Prepare a folder following the directions on page 3.

   Cover—page 7

   Student Directions—page 9

   Puzzle Pieces—pages 11–15

   Answer Key—page 17

2. Reproduce a supply of the activity sheet on page 6. Place copies in the left-hand pocket of the folder.

Partner Practice	Independent Practice
1. The students sort the puzzle pieces into three piles—words, words with pronunciations, and sentences.	1. The student sorts the puzzle pieces into three piles—words, words with pronunciations, and sentences.
2. Working together, the students make a three-part puzzle by piecing together two synonyms and the corresponding sentence.	2. The student pieces together two synonyms and the corresponding sentence to make a three-part puzzle.
3. The students repeat Step 2 to complete the other eight puzzles. Encourage the students to read aloud the three parts of each completed puzzle.	3. The student repeats Step 2 to complete the other eight puzzles. Encourage the student to read aloud the three parts of each completed puzzle.
4. Then the students work cooperatively to complete their own activity sheet.	4. Then the student completes the activity sheet.
5. Finally, the students check their work using the answer key.	5. Finally, the student self-checks by using the answer key.

Fabulous Synonyms

Complete the crossword puzzle. Find the synonym for each clue word.
Use the word box to help you.

Across	Down
1. delicate	1. loyal
3. surprised	2. thin
5. wonderful	4. lucky
6. sad	5. fussy
7. fierce	

Word Box

fabulous	flimsy
faithful	forlorn
ferocious	fortunate
finicky	fragile
flabbergasted	

    Take It to Your Seat—Vocabulary Centers • EMC 3350 • © Evan-Moor Corp.

FABULOUS SYNONYMS

Take It to Your Seat—Vocabulary Centers • EMC 3350 • © Evan-Moor Corp.

Fabulous Synonyms

Word Wiz

Synonyms are words that mean the same or nearly the same.

The words fabulous and wonderful are synonyms.
They have the same meaning.

I think it is **fabulous** that you won the contest.

I think it is **wonderful** that you won the contest.

Follow These Steps

Partner Practice

1. Sort the puzzle pieces into three piles—words, words with pronunciations, and sentences.

2. Piece together two synonyms and a sentence to complete a puzzle. Take turns reading the sentence aloud, substituting each synonym in the sentence.

3. Take turns to complete the other eight puzzles.

4. Work together to complete your own activity sheet.

5. Check your work using the answer key.

Independent Practice

1. Sort the puzzle pieces into three piles—words, words with pronunciations, and sentences.

2. Piece together two synonyms and a sentence to complete a puzzle.

3. Repeat Step 2 to complete the other eight puzzles. Read each sentence aloud, using each synonym.

4. Complete the activity sheet.

5. Check your work using the answer key.

10

fabulous
(**fab**-yuh-luhss)

wonderful

Jenny had a _____ time at the birthday party.

ferocious
(fuh-**roh**-shuhss)

fierce

The _____ lion attacked the zebra.

fragile
(**fraj**-il)

delicate

The _____ flower was easily broken by the gentle breeze.

Fabulous Synonyms

EMC 3350 • © Evan-Moor Corp.

Fabulous Synonyms

EMC 3350 • © Evan-Moor Corp.

Fabulous Synonyms

EMC 3350 • © Evan-Moor Corp.

Fabulous Synonyms

EMC 3350 • © Evan-Moor Corp.

Fabulous Synonyms

EMC 3350 • © Evan-Moor Corp.

Fabulous Synonyms

EMC 3350 • © Evan-Moor Corp.

Fabulous Synonyms

EMC 3350 • © Evan-Moor Corp.

Fabulous Synonyms

EMC 3350 • © Evan-Moor Corp.

Fabulous Synonyms

EMC 3350 • © Evan-Moor Corp.

finicky
(**fin**-uh-kee)

fussy

Mom calls Annie a _____ eater because she won't eat vegetables.

flabbergasted
(**flab**-ur-gass-tid)

surprised

Mrs. Brown was _____ to see her cat standing on its head.

fortunate
(**for**-chuh-nit)

lucky

I am _____ that my grandparents live close by.

Fabulous Synonyms

EMC 3350 • © Evan-Moor Corp.

Fabulous Synonyms

EMC 3350 • © Evan-Moor Corp.

Fabulous Synonyms

EMC 3350 • © Evan-Moor Corp.

Fabulous Synonyms

EMC 3350 • © Evan-Moor Corp.

Fabulous Synonyms

EMC 3350 • © Evan-Moor Corp.

Fabulous Synonyms

EMC 3350 • © Evan-Moor Corp.

Fabulous Synonyms

EMC 3350 • © Evan-Moor Corp.

Fabulous Synonyms

EMC 3350 • © Evan-Moor Corp.

Fabulous Synonyms

EMC 3350 • © Evan-Moor Corp.

faithful
(**fayth**-fuhl)

loyal

I can count on my best friend Joey because he is _____.

flimsy
(**flim**-zee)

thin

The _____ bag broke, spilling all our groceries.

forlorn
(for-**lorn**)

sad

When her dog was lost, Tanya felt _____.

Fabulous Synonyms

EMC 3350 • © Evan-Moor Corp.

Fabulous Synonyms

EMC 3350 • © Evan-Moor Corp.

Fabulous Synonyms

EMC 3350 • © Evan-Moor Corp.

Fabulous Synonyms

EMC 3350 • © Evan-Moor Corp.

Fabulous Synonyms

EMC 3350 • © Evan-Moor Corp.

Fabulous Synonyms

EMC 3350 • © Evan-Moor Corp.

Fabulous Synonyms

EMC 3350 • © Evan-Moor Corp.

Fabulous Synonyms

EMC 3350 • © Evan-Moor Corp.

Fabulous Synonyms

EMC 3350 • © Evan-Moor Corp.

Fabulous Synonyms

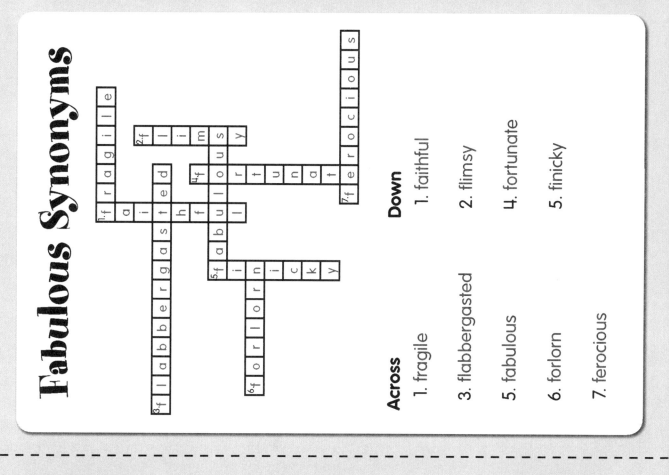

Across

1. fragile

3. flabbergasted

5. fabulous

6. forlorn

7. ferocious

Down

1. faithful

2. flimsy

4. fortunate

5. finicky

18

Antonym Bingo

Preparing the Center

1. Prepare a folder following the directions on page 3.

   Cover—page 21
   Student Directions—page 23
   Game Rules—page 25
   Game Boards—pages 27 and 29
   Clue Cards—pages 31 and 33
   Answer Key—page 35

2. Reproduce a supply of the activity sheet on page 20. Place copies in the left-hand pocket of the folder.

Partner Practice

1. The students read the game rules for two players.

2. The students decide which of them will be the leader for the game. The leader may play.

3. Each student receives a game board and some markers. (Use colored paper squares, pennies, or dried beans for markers.)

4. The students follow the rules to play Antonym Bingo.

5. Then students work cooperatively to complete their own activity sheet.

6. Finally, the students check their work using the answer key.

Independent Practice

1. The student reads the game rules for one player.

2. The student takes a game board and some markers. (Use colored paper squares, pennies, or dried beans for markers.)

3. The student follows the rules to play Antonym Bingo.

4. Then the student completes the activity sheet.

5. Finally, the student self-checks by using the answer key.

Antonym Bingo

Circle the correct antonym to complete each sentence.

1. The teacher was happy because all of the students were **(absent, present)** for picture day.

2. The little children were told to play in the **(deep, shallow)** end of the pool.

3. The **(maximum, minimum)** speed limit on the highway is 65 miles per hour.

4. Sammie got lost because the directions on the map were **(simple, complex)**.

5. Many ships can sail on the **(broad, narrow)** ocean.

6. My grandpa is **(generous, stingy)** because he gives me great birthday presents.

7. It is **(polite, rude)** to interrupt when someone is speaking.

8. To see a two-headed snake is a **(common, rare)** event.

9. The wonderful bakery serves only **(fresh, stale)** bagels.

10. The sound of her **(gentle, harsh)** voice hurt my ears.

11. The **(public, private)** library was open to everyone in the city.

12. I had to wait because the restroom was already **(occupied, vacant)**.

ANTONYM BINGO

Antonyms are words that have opposite meanings.

Hot and **cold** are antonyms.

Innocent and **guilty** are antonyms.

Follow These Steps

Partner Practice

1. Both players take a game board and some markers.

2. Take turns reading the bingo rules for two players.

3. Play Antonym Bingo.

4. Work together to complete your own activity sheet.

5. Check your work using the answer key.

Independent Practice

1. Take a game board, some markers, and the clue cards.

2. Read the bingo rules for one player.

3. Play Antonym Bingo.

4. Complete the activity sheet.

5. Check your work using the answer key.

Rules for 2 Players:

1. Choose a leader to read the clue cards. The leader also plays.

2. Shuffle the clue cards and stack them clue side up.

3. Take a bingo card and some markers. Place a marker on the FREE space.

4. The leader reads aloud the top clue card and sets it aside to use for checking.

5. Find the antonym, or opposite, on your game board and cover the word with a marker.

6. Repeat the process until one player covers a row horizontally, vertically, or diagonally. That player calls out, "Antonym Bingo!"

7. The leader checks the words covered on the game board against the answers on the backs of the clue cards.

8. If the antonyms match, the player wins and becomes the leader for the next round.

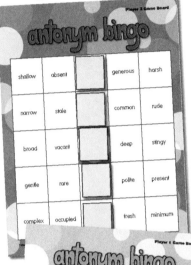

Rules for 1 Player:

1. Shuffle the clue cards and stack them clue side up.

2. Take a bingo card and some markers. Place a marker on the FREE space.

3. Read the top clue card. Set the card aside to use for checking.

4. Place a marker on the matching antonym.

5. Continue playing until you have a bingo, or five in a row. The row may be horizontal, vertical, or diagonal.

6. Check the words covered on the game board against the answers on the backs of the clue cards.

antonym bingo

absent	shallow	maximum	simple	broad
generous	polite	common	fresh	gentle
harsh	deep	FREE	private	vacant
narrow	minimum	rude	complex	stingy
stale	rare	occupied	present	public

Take It to Your Seat—Vocabulary Centers • EMC 3350 • © Evan-Moor Corp.

antonym bingo

shallow	absent	private	generous	harsh
narrow	stale	maximum	common	rude
broad	vacant	**FREE**	deep	stingy
gentle	rare	public	polite	present
complex	occupied	simple	fresh	minimum

the opposite of **absent**

the opposite of **shallow**

the opposite of **private**

the opposite of **generous**

the opposite of **harsh**

the opposite of **narrow**

the opposite of **stale**

the opposite of **maximum**

the opposite of **common**

the opposite of **rude**

the opposite of **vacant**

the opposite of **complex**

public

deep

present

broad

gentle

stingy

rare

minimum

fresh

simple

occupied

polite

the opposite of **present**

the opposite of **deep**

the opposite of **public**

the opposite of **stingy**

the opposite of **gentle**

the opposite of **broad**

the opposite of **fresh**

the opposite of **minimum**

the opposite of **rare**

the opposite of **polite**

the opposite of **occupied**

the opposite of **simple**

private

Antonym Bingo

EMC 3350 • © Evan-Moor Corp.

shallow

Antonym Bingo

EMC 3350 • © Evan-Moor Corp.

absent

Antonym Bingo

EMC 3350 • © Evan-Moor Corp.

narrow

Antonym Bingo

EMC 3350 • © Evan-Moor Corp.

harsh

Antonym Bingo

EMC 3350 • © Evan-Moor Corp.

generous

Antonym Bingo

EMC 3350 • © Evan-Moor Corp.

common

Antonym Bingo

EMC 3350 • © Evan-Moor Corp.

maximum

Antonym Bingo

EMC 3350 • © Evan-Moor Corp.

stale

Antonym Bingo

EMC 3350 • © Evan-Moor Corp.

complex

Antonym Bingo

EMC 3350 • © Evan-Moor Corp.

vacant

Antonym Bingo

EMC 3350 • © Evan-Moor Corp.

rude

Antonym Bingo

EMC 3350 • © Evan-Moor Corp.

Antonym Bingo

1. The teacher was happy because all of the students were **(absent, present)** for picture day.

2. The little children were told to play in the **(deep, shallow)** end of the pool.

3. The **(maximum, minimum)** speed limit on the highway is 65 miles per hour.

4. Sammie got lost because the directions on the map were **(simple, complex)**.

5. Many ships can sail on the **(broad, narrow)** ocean.

6. My grandpa is **(generous, stingy)** because he gives me great birthday presents.

7. It is **(polite, rude)** to interrupt when someone is speaking.

8. To see a two-headed snake is a **(common, rare)** event.

9. The wonderful bakery serves only **(fresh, stale)** bagels.

10. The sound of her **(gentle, harsh)** voice hurt my ears.

11. The **(public, private)** library was open to everyone in the city.

12. I had to wait because the restroom was already **(occupied, vacant)**.

Answer Key

ANTONYM BINGO

Lift the flap to check your answers.

Homophone Match

Preparing the Center

1. Prepare a folder following the directions on page 3.

   Cover—page 39

   Student Directions—page 41

   Game Rules—page 43

   Playing Cards—pages 45–51

   Answer Key—page 53

2. Reproduce a supply of the activity sheet on page 38. Place copies in the left-hand pocket of the folder.

Partner Practice

1. The students read the game rules for two players. This homophone card game is similar to the familiar children's game Old Maid.

2. The students play Hoarse Horse. Encourage the students to read aloud each pair of sentences.

3. Then the students work cooperatively to complete their own activity sheet.

4. Finally, the students check their work using the answer key.

Independent Practice

1. The student reads the game rules for one player. This homophone card game is similar to the familiar children's game Concentration.

2. The student plays Hoarse Horse. After each match, the student reads aloud the words and sentences in the homophone pair.

3. Then the student completes the activity sheet.

4. Finally, the student self-checks by using the answer key.

Homophone Match

Write the matching homophones on the lines.

1. hole   __ ◯ __ __ __

2. doe   __ ◯ __ __ __

3. hare   __ ◯ __ __

4. flower   __ __ __ __ ◯

5. rose   __ __ __ ◯

6. mail   __ __ __ ◯

7. knight   __ __ __ ◯ __

8. chord   __ ◯ __ __

9. fare   __ __ __ ◯

10. sail   ◯ __ __ __

11. tail   __ __ __ ◯

Write the circled letters in order on the lines below to answer the riddle.

What do you call a hoofed animal that has a sore throat?

a   __ __ __ __ __ __   __ __ __ __ __

Take It to Your Seat—Vocabulary Centers • EMC 3350 • © Evan-Moor Corp.

HOMOPHONE MATCH

Word Wiz

Homophones are two words that sound alike but have different spellings and different meanings.

Hoarse and horse are homophones.

Hoarse means to have a low, rough voice.

A **horse** is a hoofed animal.

Follow These Steps

Partner Practice

1. Take turns reading the game rules for two players.

2. Play Hoarse Horse.

3. Work together to complete your own activity sheet.

4. Check your work using the answer key.

Independent Practice

1. Read the game rules for one player.

2. Play Hoarse Horse.

3. Complete the activity sheet.

4. Check your work using the answer key.

Rules for 2 Players:

This game is played like the card game Old Maid.

1. The players choose a dealer. The dealer shuffles the cards. The dealer gives one card at a time to both players until all the cards are dealt.

2. The players place all their matching homophone pairs faceup on the table, and hold on to the rest.

3. The dealer picks a card from the other player. If it matches a card in the dealer's hand, the dealer places the homophone pair faceup on the table. If it does not make a match, the dealer holds on to the card.

4. The second player selects a card from the dealer and does the same.

5. The game continues until all homophone pairs have been matched. The player who is left with the Hoarse Horse card loses the game.

6. The two players read the homophone pairs and their definitions to each other.

Rules for 1 Player:

This game is played like the game Concentration.

1. Set the Hoarse Horse card aside. Shuffle the rest of the cards.

2. Spread out the cards facedown on the table. The cards should be close together, but they should not overlap.

3. Select two cards and turn them faceup. If the cards are matching homophones, take them. If the two cards do not match, turn them back over.

4. Read the words and sentences in the pair each time you make a match.

5. Keep playing until you have matched all 11 pairs of homophones.

hole

There was a **hole** in the boy's shirt.

whole

The boy ate the **whole** sandwich.

tail

The fox has a beautiful **tail**.

tale

The **tale** of the fox and the hound was exciting to read.

doe

The **doe** watched over her fawn.

dough

She kneaded the **dough** to make a loaf of bread.

Homophone Match

EMC 3350 • © Evan-Moor Corp.

Homophone Match

EMC 3350 • © Evan-Moor Corp.

Homophone Match

EMC 3350 • © Evan-Moor Corp.

Homophone Match

EMC 3350 • © Evan-Moor Corp.

Homophone Match

EMC 3350 • © Evan-Moor Corp.

Homophone Match

EMC 3350 • © Evan-Moor Corp.

hare

The **hare** munched on some lettuce.

hair

Her **hair** was so long that she could put a bow in it.

knight

The brave **knight** was ready for battle.

night

The warrior stood guard all **night** long.

rose

I will pick a red **rose** for my mother.

rows

The flower bushes were planted in two **rows**.

Homophone Match

EMC 3350 • © Evan-Moor Corp.

Homophone Match

EMC 3350 • © Evan-Moor Corp.

Homophone Match

EMC 3350 • © Evan-Moor Corp.

Homophone Match

EMC 3350 • © Evan-Moor Corp.

Homophone Match

EMC 3350 • © Evan-Moor Corp.

Homophone Match

EMC 3350 • © Evan-Moor Corp.

fair

Our family went on the Ferris wheel at the county **fair**.

fare

The **fare** to ride the Ferris wheel is $1.50.

flour

Natalie will use the whole bag of **flour** to make cookies.

flower

Natalie loves the **flower** her daughter gave her.

male

The **male** lion has a large mane around his neck.

mail

George likes to read the **mail** as soon as it arrives.

Homophone Match

EMC 3350 • © Evan-Moor Corp.

Homophone Match

EMC 3350 • © Evan-Moor Corp.

Homophone Match

EMC 3350 • © Evan-Moor Corp.

Homophone Match

EMC 3350 • © Evan-Moor Corp.

Homophone Match

EMC 3350 • © Evan-Moor Corp.

Homophone Match

EMC 3350 • © Evan-Moor Corp.

cord

I plug the **cord** into the wall so I can play my guitar.

chord

I strummed three notes together and played a musical **chord**.

sail

The **sail** caught the wind, and the boat sped away across the lake.

sale

The boy put a price tag on his boat because it was for **sale**.

Hoarse Horse

Homophone Match

EMC 3350 • © Evan-Moor Corp.

Homophone Match

EMC 3350 • © Evan-Moor Corp.

Homophone Match

EMC 3350 • © Evan-Moor Corp.

Homophone Match

EMC 3350 • © Evan-Moor Corp.

Homophone Match

EMC 3350 • © Evan-Moor Corp.

Homophone Match

1. hole   w(h)o l e
2. doe   d(o)u g h
3. hare   h(ai)r
4. flower   f l o u(r)
5. rose   r o w(s)
6. mail   m a l(e)
7. knight   n i g(h)t
8. chord   c(h)o r d
9. fare   f a i(r)
10. sail   (s)a l e
11. tail   t a l(e)

What do you call a hoofed animal that has a sore throat?

a h o a r s e   h o r s e

HOMOPHONE MATCH

Lift the flap to check your answers.

54

Prefix Preview

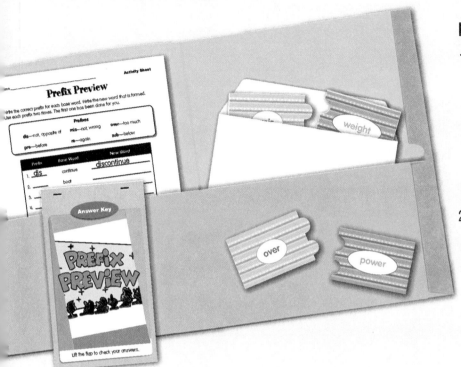

Preparing the Center

1. Prepare a folder following the directions on page 3.

   Cover—page 57

   Student Directions—page 59

   Puzzle Pieces—pages 61–65

   Answer Key—page 67

2. Reproduce a supply of the activity sheet on page 56. Place copies in the left-hand pocket of the folder.

Partner Practice	Independent Practice
1. The students sort the puzzle pieces into two piles—prefixes and base words.	1. The student sorts the puzzle pieces into two piles—prefixes and base words.
2. Working together, the students fit together a prefix and a base word to form a new word. The students read aloud the new word and define it. They then turn the puzzle over and read the definition and the sentence that uses the word.	2. The student fits together a prefix and a base word to form a new word. The student reads aloud the new word and defines it. The student turns the puzzle over to read the definition and the sentence that uses the word.
3. The students repeat Step 2 to complete the other 11 puzzles.	3. The student repeats Step 2 to complete the other 11 puzzles.
4. Then the students work cooperatively to complete their own activity sheet.	4. Then the student completes the activity sheet.
5. Finally, the students check their work using the answer key.	5. Finally, the student self-checks by using the answer key.

Prefix Preview

Write the correct prefix for each base word. Write the new word that is formed.
Use each prefix two times. The first one has been done for you.

Prefixes

dis—not, opposite of   **mis**—not, wrong   **over**—too much

pre—before   **re**—again   **sub**—below

Prefix	Base Word	New Word
1. dis	continue	discontinue
2. ____	boot	____
3. ____	weight	____
4. ____	lead	____
5. ____	obey	____
6. ____	way	____
7. ____	trace	____
8. ____	behave	____
9. ____	merge	____
10. ____	school	____
11. ____	power	____
12. ____	historic	____

Prefix Preview
Student Directions

A **prefix** is a word part that is added to the beginning of a word. When you add a prefix, you change the word's meaning.

prefix	+	base word	=	new word
dis	+	connect	=	disconnect
(not, opposite of)		(to join)		(to separate)

Common Prefixes

dis—not, opposite of   **mis**—not, wrong   **over**—too much
pre—before   **re**—again   **sub**—below

Follow These Steps

Partner Practice

1. Sort the puzzle pieces into two piles—prefixes and base words.

2. Working together, fit the prefixes to the correct base words to form 12 new words.

3. Take turns reading the new words aloud and telling what they mean. Turn the puzzles over to read the definition and the sentence.

4. Work together to complete your own activity sheet.

5. Check your work using the answer key.

Independent Practice

1. Sort the puzzle pieces into two piles—prefixes and base words.

2. Fit a prefix to the correct base word to create a new word.

3. Read the new word aloud and think about its meaning. Turn the puzzle over to read the definition and the sentence.

4. Repeat Steps 2 and 3 to form the other 11 new words.

5. Complete the activity sheet.

6. Check your work using the answer key.

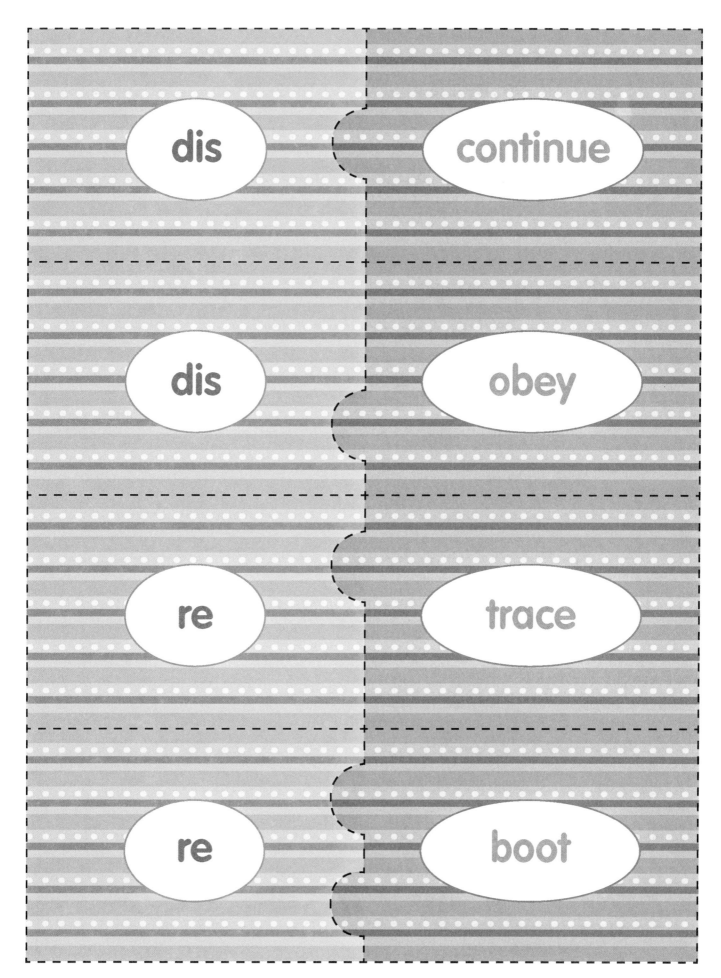

dis continue

dis obey

re trace

re boot

To **discontinue** means to stop something from continuing.

We will **discontinue** our mail service while we are on vacation.

If you **disobey,** you do not do as you are told.

Some drivers **disobey** a red light and drive through it.

To **retrace** is to go back over something again.

I had to **retrace** my steps to find my lost ring.

To **reboot** is to start a computer again.

Joe will **reboot** his computer after he installs the new program.

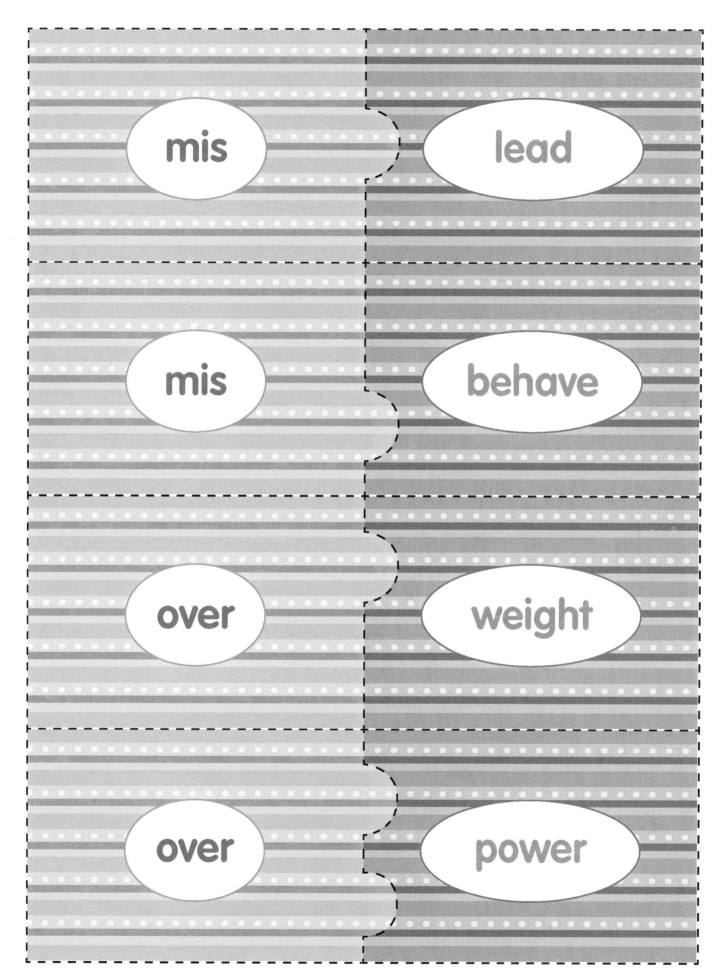

mis · lead

mis · behave

over · weight

over · power

To **mislead** is to give someone the wrong idea about something.

The confusing signs tend to **mislead** us.

To **misbehave** is to do what should not be done.

If you **misbehave** in the library, you will be sent home.

To be **overweight** means to weigh too much.

An **overweight** person's heart works very hard
to pump blood through the body.

To **overpower** is to defeat someone because
you are stronger than the other person.

The big wrestler will **overpower** the smaller man.

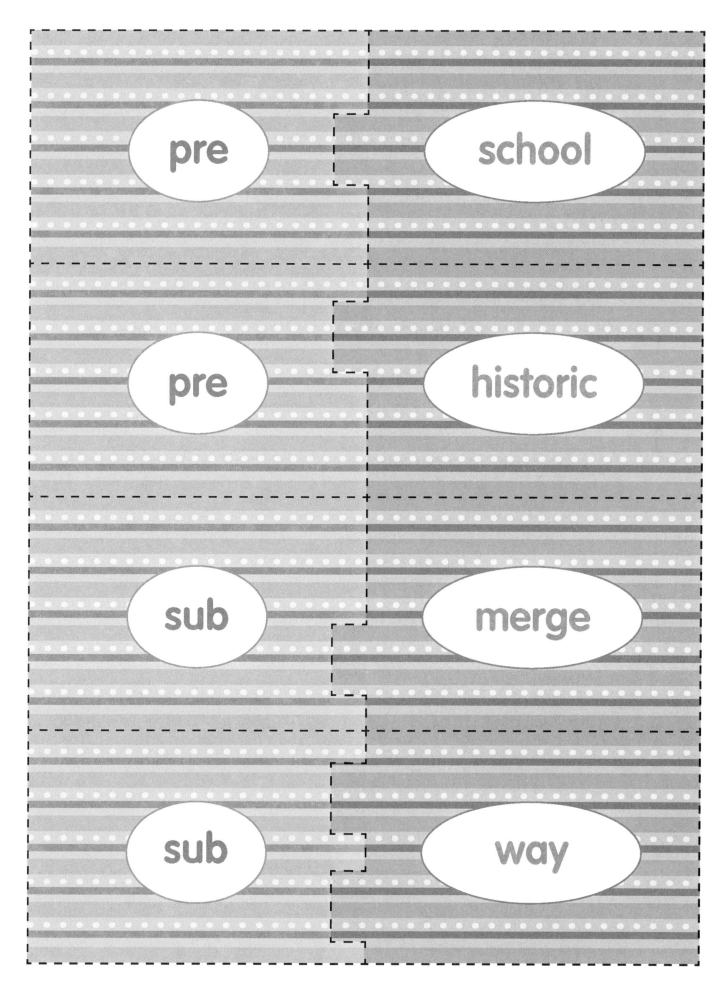

pre · school

pre · historic

sub · merge

sub · way

Preschool comes before kindergarten.

My sister takes a nap every day while she's in **preschool**.

Prefix Preview
EMC 3350 • © Evan-Moor Corp.

Prefix Preview
EMC 3350 • © Evan-Moor Corp.

Things that are **prehistoric** happened before events in history were written down.

Dinosaurs were **prehistoric** animals that lived on Earth before people.

Prefix Preview
EMC 3350 • © Evan-Moor Corp.

Prefix Preview
EMC 3350 • © Evan-Moor Corp.

To **submerge** is to sink or plunge below the surface of water or another liquid.

I like to **submerge** myself in the cool lake.

Prefix Preview
EMC 3350 • © Evan-Moor Corp.

Prefix Preview
EMC 3350 • © Evan-Moor Corp.

A **subway** is a railway below the ground.

Go down these stairs to get to the **subway** station.

Prefix Preview
EMC 3350 • © Evan-Moor Corp.

Prefix Preview
EMC 3350 • © Evan-Moor Corp.

Prefix Preview

	Prefix	Base Word	New Word
1.	dis	continue	discontinue
2.	re	boot	reboot
3.	over	weight	overweight
4.	mis	lead	mislead
5.	dis	obey	disobey
6.	sub	way	subway
7.	re	trace	retrace
8.	mis	behave	misbehave
9.	sub	merge	submerge
10.	pre	school	preschool
11.	over	power	overpower
12.	pre	historic	prehistoric

Lift the flap to check your answers.

Working Suffixes

Preparing the Center

1. Prepare a folder following the directions on page 3.

    Cover—page 71

    Student Directions—page 73

    Task Cards—pages 75–81

    Answer Key—page 83

2. Reproduce a supply of the activity sheet on page 70. Place copies in the left-hand pocket of the folder.

Partner Practice

1. The students sort the task cards into three piles—base words, suffixes (-*er* and -*or*), and job descriptions.

2. Working together, the students match the base words (verbs) with the correct suffix to form new words (nouns). The nouns are types of workers.

3. The students then match the workers with their job descriptions. The students turn the job description cards over to check their work.

4. Then the students work cooperatively to complete their own activity sheet.

5. Finally, the students check their work using the answer key.

Independent Practice

1. The student sorts the task cards into three piles—base words, suffixes (-*er* and -*or*), and job descriptions.

2. The student matches the base words (verbs) with the correct suffix to form new words (nouns). The nouns are types of workers.

3. The student matches the workers with their job descriptions. The student turns the job description cards over to check his or her work.

4. Then the student completes the activity sheet.

5. Finally, the student self-checks by using the answer key.

Working Suffixes

Unscramble the letters in the parentheses ( ) to spell a word that makes sense in each sentence. The first letter of the word is boldfaced.

1. The _____ fixed the errors in the book before it was published.
   (rotdi**e**)

2. The _____ gave a wonderful talk at the church service.
   (er**p**rahce)

3. The _____ handed out the assignment to the students.
   (tcurtron**i**s)

4. The _____ led the orchestra in playing beautiful music.
   (dutcnoor**c**)

5. The _____ checked the elevators to make sure they were safe.
   (**c**epsnirot)

6. The _____ sent out an emergency call for more firefighters.
   (pahcsi**d**ret)

7. The _____ translated the speech into French.
   (erpreter**t**in)

8. The _____ took amazing pictures of African lions.
   (h**p**argotohpre)

9. The _____ melted two pipes so they could be joined together.
   (dle**w**er)

10. The _____ listened to her problems and gave her good advice.
    (se**c**oonulr)

11. The _____ made sketches for a new line of clothing.
    (sign**d**eer)

12. The _____ carved an impressive statue out of stone.
    (plus**c**tro)

    Take It to Your Seat—Vocabulary Centers • EMC 3350 • © Evan-Moor Corp.

Working Suffixes

Word Wiz

A **suffix** is a word part that comes at the end of a base word.
When you add a suffix, you change the word's meaning.

The suffixes **-er** and **-or** change the base words from verbs to nouns.

-er and **-or** mean "a person who"

teach + **er** = teacher

OR

invent + **or** = inventor
(verb) + (suffix) = (noun)

Follow These Steps

Partner Practice

1. Sort the cards into three piles—base words, suffixes, and job descriptions.

2. Working together, match the base word with the correct suffix to make a new word. The new word is a type of worker.

3. Then match the worker with its job description. Turn the job description card over to check your work.

4. Repeat Steps 2 and 3 to match the other 11 workers with their jobs.

5. Work together to complete your own activity sheet.

6. Check your work using the answer key.

Independent Practice

1. Sort the cards into three piles—base words, suffixes, and job descriptions.

2. Match the base word with the correct suffix to make a new word. The new word is a type of worker.

3. Then match the worker with its job description. Turn the job description card over to check your work.

4. Repeat Steps 2 and 3 to match the other 11 workers with their jobs.

5. Complete the activity sheet.

6. Check your work using the answer key.

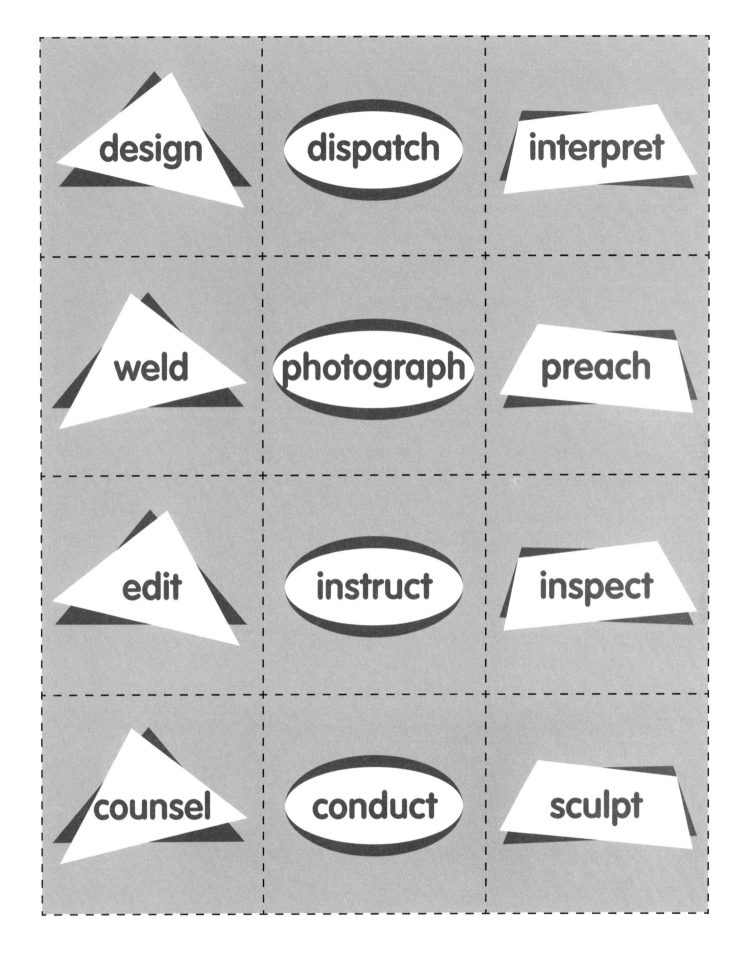

design

dispatch

interpret

weld

photograph

preach

edit

instruct

inspect

counsel

conduct

sculpt

Working Suffixes

EMC 3350 • © Evan-Moor Corp.

Working Suffixes

EMC 3350 • © Evan-Moor Corp.

Working Suffixes

EMC 3350 • © Evan-Moor Corp.

Working Suffixes

EMC 3350 • © Evan-Moor Corp.

Working Suffixes

EMC 3350 • © Evan-Moor Corp.

Working Suffixes

EMC 3350 • © Evan-Moor Corp.

Working Suffixes

EMC 3350 • © Evan-Moor Corp.

Working Suffixes

EMC 3350 • © Evan-Moor Corp.

Working Suffixes

EMC 3350 • © Evan-Moor Corp.

Working Suffixes

EMC 3350 • © Evan-Moor Corp.

Working Suffixes

EMC 3350 • © Evan-Moor Corp.

Working Suffixes

EMC 3350 • © Evan-Moor Corp.

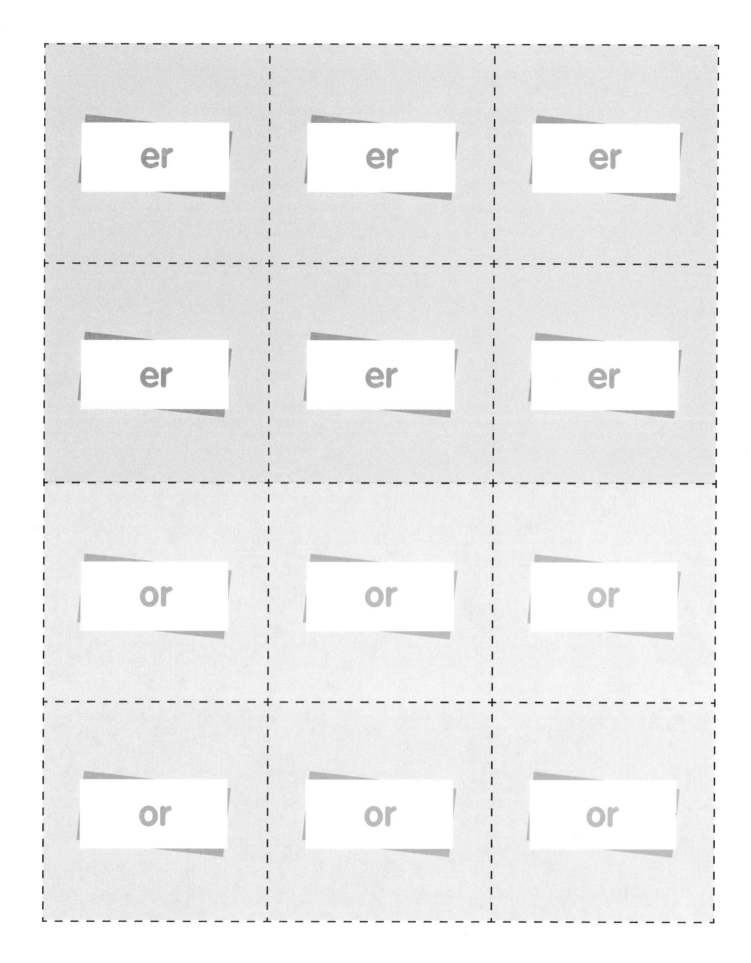

Working Suffixes

EMC 3350 • © Evan-Moor Corp.

Working Suffixes

EMC 3350 • © Evan-Moor Corp.

Working Suffixes

EMC 3350 • © Evan-Moor Corp.

Working Suffixes

EMC 3350 • © Evan-Moor Corp.

Working Suffixes

EMC 3350 • © Evan-Moor Corp.

Working Suffixes

EMC 3350 • © Evan-Moor Corp.

Working Suffixes

EMC 3350 • © Evan-Moor Corp.

Working Suffixes

EMC 3350 • © Evan-Moor Corp.

Working Suffixes

EMC 3350 • © Evan-Moor Corp.

Working Suffixes

EMC 3350 • © Evan-Moor Corp.

Working Suffixes

EMC 3350 • © Evan-Moor Corp.

Working Suffixes

EMC 3350 • © Evan-Moor Corp.

a worker who draws something
that could be built or made

a worker who sends out important
messages to people

a worker who translates what is said from
one language to another

a worker who heats two pieces of metal or plastic
until they are soft enough to be joined together

a worker who takes pictures using a camera,
and then develops them

a worker who gives a religious talk to people,
especially during a church service

design + er = designer

Working Suffixes

EMC 3350 • © Evan-Moor Corp.

dispatch + er = dispatcher

Working Suffixes

EMC 3350 • © Evan-Moor Corp.

interpret + er = interpreter

Working Suffixes

EMC 3350 • © Evan-Moor Corp.

weld + er = welder

Working Suffixes

EMC 3350 • © Evan-Moor Corp.

photograph + er = photographer

Working Suffixes

EMC 3350 • © Evan-Moor Corp.

preach + er = preacher

Working Suffixes

EMC 3350 • © Evan-Moor Corp.

a worker who checks the contents of a book and gets it ready to be published

a worker who teaches a subject or a skill

a worker who checks or examines things to make sure they are safe to use

a worker who helps people with their problems and gives them advice

a worker who directs a group of musicians while they play

a worker who carves or shapes stone, wood, metal, marble, or clay to make an art piece

edit + or = editor

Working Suffixes

EMC 3350 • © Evan-Moor Corp.

instruct + or = instructor

Working Suffixes

EMC 3350 • © Evan-Moor Corp.

inspect + or = inspector

Working Suffixes

EMC 3350 • © Evan-Moor Corp.

counsel + or = counselor

Working Suffixes

EMC 3350 • © Evan-Moor Corp.

conduct + or = conductor

Working Suffixes

EMC 3350 • © Evan-Moor Corp.

sculpt + or = sculptor

Working Suffixes

EMC 3350 • © Evan-Moor Corp.

Working Suffixes

1. editor
2. preacher
3. instructor
4. conductor
5. inspector
6. dispatcher
7. interpreter
8. photographer
9. welder
10. counselor
11. designer
12. sculptor

Lift the flap to check your answers.

84

Animal Analogies

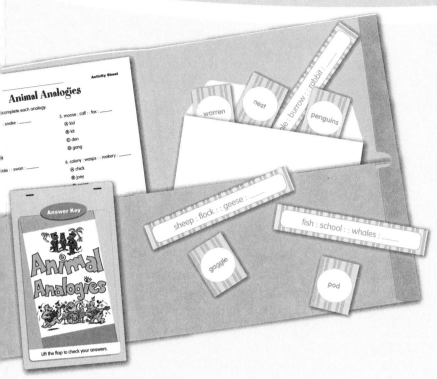

Preparing the Center

1. Prepare a folder following the directions on page 3.

   Cover—page 87

   Student Directions—page 89

   Task Cards—pages 91–95

   Answer Key—page 97

2. Reproduce a supply of the activity sheet on page 86. Place copies in the left-hand pocket of the folder.

Partner Practice

1. The students sort the task cards into two piles—analogy starters and words. The students practice three kinds of animal analogies—*group : members, animal : home,* and *adult : offspring.*

2. Working together, the students read aloud an analogy starter and complete it with the correct word card. The cards are self-checking on the back.

3. The students repeat Step 2 to match the other 15 analogies.

4. Then the students work cooperatively to complete their own activity sheet.

5. Finally, the students check their work using the answer key.

Independent Practice

1. The student sorts the task cards into two piles—analogy starters and words. The student practices three kinds of animal analogies—*group : members, animal : home,* and *adult : offspring.*

2. The student reads aloud an analogy starter and completes it with the correct word card. The student turns the cards over to check the answer.

3. The student repeats Step 2 to match the other 15 analogies.

4. Then the student completes the activity sheet.

5. Finally, the student self-checks by using the answer key.

Animal Analogies

Fill in the circle to complete each analogy.

1. spider : web : : snake : _____
   - Ⓐ band
   - Ⓑ nest
   - Ⓒ reptile
   - Ⓓ hatchling

2. frog : tadpole : : swan : _____
   - Ⓐ cygnet
   - Ⓑ chick
   - Ⓒ team
   - Ⓓ flight

3. gorillas : band : : monkeys : _____
   - Ⓐ cub
   - Ⓑ infant
   - Ⓒ mob
   - Ⓓ troop

4. ant : hill : : termite : _____
   - Ⓐ insect
   - Ⓑ swarm
   - Ⓒ mound
   - Ⓓ larva

5. moose : calf : : fox : _____
   - Ⓐ kid
   - Ⓑ kit
   - Ⓒ den
   - Ⓓ gang

6. colony : wasps : : rookery : _____
   - Ⓐ chick
   - Ⓑ joey
   - Ⓒ geese
   - Ⓓ penguins

7. bear : den : : beaver : _____
   - Ⓐ lodge
   - Ⓑ roost
   - Ⓒ pup
   - Ⓓ cub

8. mole : burrow : : rabbit : _____
   - Ⓐ bunny
   - Ⓑ mound
   - Ⓒ warren
   - Ⓓ school

Animal Analogies

Animal Analogies
Student Directions

An **analogy** is a comparison that shows the relationship between two pairs of words.

Three Kinds of Analogies

1

Group Name and Members of the Group

herd : cattle : : pride : lions

(**herd** is to **cattle** as **pride** is to **lions**)

2

Animal Name and Its Home

bird : nest : : bee : hive

(**bird** is to **nest** as **bee** is to **hive**)

3

Adult Animal and Its Offspring (baby)

cat : kitten : : dog : pup

(**cat** is to **kitten** as **dog** is to **pup**)

Follow These Steps

Partner Practice

1. Sort the cards into two piles—analogy starters and word cards.

2. Read an analogy card. Find the word card that completes the analogy. Take turns reading the analogy to each other. Turn the two cards over to check your work.

3. Repeat Step 2 to complete the other 15 analogies.

4. Work together to complete your own activity sheet.

5. Check your work using the answer key.

Independent Practice

1. Sort the cards into two piles—analogy starters and word cards.

2. Read an analogy card. Find the word card that completes the analogy. Read the analogy aloud. Turn the two cards over to check your work.

3. Repeat Step 2 to complete the other 15 analogies.

4. Complete the activity sheet.

5. Check your work using the answer key.

sheep : flock : : geese : _____

fish : school : : whales : _____

gang : elk : : mob : _____

gorillas : band : : monkeys : _____

colony : wasps : : rookery : _____

bear : den : : beaver : _____

ant : hill : : termite : _____

mole : burrow : : rabbit : _____

Animal Analogies

EMC 3350 • © Evan-Moor Corp.

Animal Analogies

EMC 3350 • © Evan-Moor Corp.

Animal Analogies

EMC 3350 • © Evan-Moor Corp.

Animal Analogies

EMC 3350 • © Evan-Moor Corp.

Animal Analogies

EMC 3350 • © Evan-Moor Corp.

Animal Analogies

EMC 3350 • © Evan-Moor Corp.

Animal Analogies

EMC 3350 • © Evan-Moor Corp.

Animal Analogies

EMC 3350 • © Evan-Moor Corp.

spider : web : : snake : ____

bee : hive : : bat : ____

deer : fawn : : koala : ____

sheep : lamb : : goat : ____

duck : duckling : : turtle : ____

frog : tadpole : : swan : ____

bear : cub : : horse : ____

moose : calf : : fox : ____

Animal Analogies

EMC 3350 • © Evan-Moor Corp.

Animal Analogies

EMC 3350 • © Evan-Moor Corp.

Animal Analogies

EMC 3350 • © Evan-Moor Corp.

Animal Analogies

EMC 3350 • © Evan-Moor Corp.

Animal Analogies

EMC 3350 • © Evan-Moor Corp.

Animal Analogies

EMC 3350 • © Evan-Moor Corp.

Animal Analogies

EMC 3350 • © Evan-Moor Corp.

Animal Analogies

EMC 3350 • © Evan-Moor Corp.

gaggle

pod

kangaroos

troop

penguins

lodge

mound

warren

nest

roost

joey

kid

hatchling

cygnet

foal

kit

Animal Analogies

EMC 3350
© Evan-Moor Corp.

Animal Analogies

EMC 3350
© Evan-Moor Corp.

Animal Analogies

EMC 3350
© Evan-Moor Corp.

Animal Analogies

EMC 3350
© Evan-Moor Corp.

Animal Analogies

EMC 3350
© Evan-Moor Corp.

Animal Analogies

EMC 3350
© Evan-Moor Corp.

Animal Analogies

EMC 3350
© Evan-Moor Corp.

Animal Analogies

EMC 3350
© Evan-Moor Corp.

Animal Analogies

EMC 3350
© Evan-Moor Corp.

Animal Analogies

EMC 3350
© Evan-Moor Corp.

Animal Analogies

EMC 3350
© Evan-Moor Corp.

Animal Analogies

EMC 3350
© Evan-Moor Corp.

Animal Analogies

EMC 3350
© Evan-Moor Corp.

Animal Analogies

EMC 3350
© Evan-Moor Corp.

Animal Analogies

EMC 3350
© Evan-Moor Corp.

Animal Analogies

EMC 3350
© Evan-Moor Corp.

Animal Analogies

1. B—nest
2. A—cygnet
3. D—troop
4. C—mound
5. B—kit
6. D—penguins
7. A—lodge
8. C—warren

Lift the flap to check your answers.

Geography Compound Words

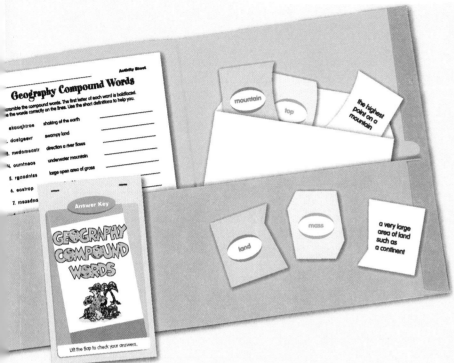

Preparing the Center

1. Prepare a folder following the directions on page 3.

    Cover—page 101

    Student Directions—page 103

    Puzzle Pieces—pages 105–111

    Answer Key—page 113

2. Reproduce a supply of the activity sheet on page 100. Place copies in the left-hand pocket of the folder.

Partner Practice

1. The students sort the puzzle pieces into three piles—blue words, green words, and definitions.

2. Working together, the students fit together two words that form a compound word and the corresponding definition of that word.

3. The students repeat Step 2 to complete the other 11 puzzles. Encourage the students to read aloud each geography compound word and definition.

4. Then the students work cooperatively to complete their own activity sheet.

5. Finally, the students check their work using the answer key.

Independent Practice

1. The student sorts the puzzle pieces into three piles—blue words, green words, and definitions.

2. The student fits together two words that form a compound word and the corresponding definition of that word.

3. The student repeats Step 2 to complete the other 11 puzzles. Encourage the student to read aloud each geography compound word and definition.

4. Then the student completes the activity sheet.

5. Finally, the student self-checks by using the answer key.

Geography Compound Words

Unscramble the compound words. The first letter of each word is boldfaced.
Write the words correctly on the lines. Use the short definitions to help you.

1. **e**kauqhtrae   shaking of the earth   _____

2. daelg**e**evr   swampy land   _____

3. nw**d**omeastr   direction a river flows   _____

4. oumtnea**s**   underwater mountain   _____

5. rg**a**adnlss   large open area of grass   _____

6. ea**s**trop   harbor for ships   _____

7. msasdna**l**   continent   _____

8. edsi**c**onurty   land away from a town or city _____

9. potniatnuo**m**   highest point on a mountain _____

10. frnottrew**a**   land located by water   _____

11. dalnelba**t**   plateau   _____

12. plooh**w**ril   water that moves in a circle _____

GEOGRAPHY COMPOUND WORDS

WORLD OR BUST

Geography Compound Words

A **compound word** is a word
made up of two smaller words.

The two smaller words **earth** and **quake** are combined
to make the compound word **earthquake**.

Follow These Steps

Partner Practice

1. Sort the puzzle pieces into three piles—blue words, green words, and definitions.

2. Fit together a blue word and a green word to form a compound word. Add the definition of the compound word to complete the three-part puzzle.

3. Take turns to complete the other 11 puzzles. Read aloud each compound word and its definition.

4. Work together to complete your own activity sheet.

5. Check your work using the answer key.

Independent Practice

1. Sort the puzzle pieces into three piles—blue words, green words, and definitions.

2. Fit together a blue word and a green word to form a compound word. Add the definition of the compound word to complete the three-part puzzle.

3. Complete the other 11 puzzles. Read aloud each compound word and its definition.

4. Complete the activity sheet.

5. Check your work using the answer key.

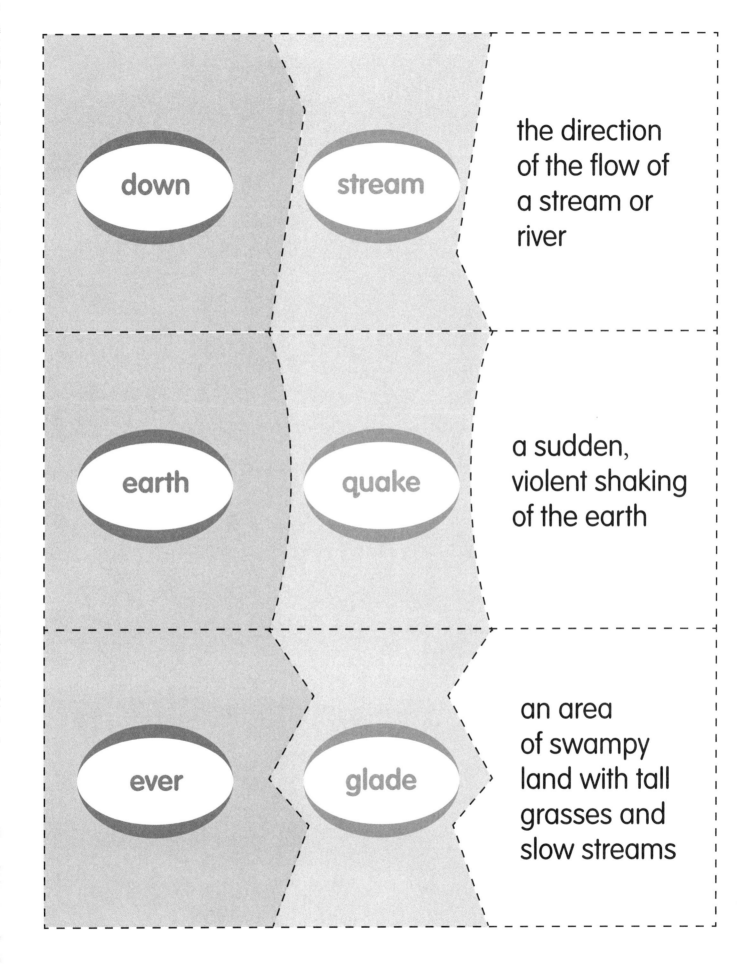

down stream — the direction of the flow of a stream or river

earth quake — a sudden, violent shaking of the earth

ever glade — an area of swampy land with tall grasses and slow streams

**Geography
Compound Words**

EMC 3350
© Evan-Moor Corp.

**Geography
Compound Words**

EMC 3350
© Evan-Moor Corp.

**Geography
Compound Words**

EMC 3350
© Evan-Moor Corp.

**Geography
Compound Words**

EMC 3350
© Evan-Moor Corp.

**Geography
Compound Words**

EMC 3350
© Evan-Moor Corp.

**Geography
Compound Words**

EMC 3350
© Evan-Moor Corp.

**Geography
Compound Words**

EMC 3350
© Evan-Moor Corp.

**Geography
Compound Words**

EMC 3350
© Evan-Moor Corp.

**Geography
Compound Words**

EMC 3350
© Evan-Moor Corp.

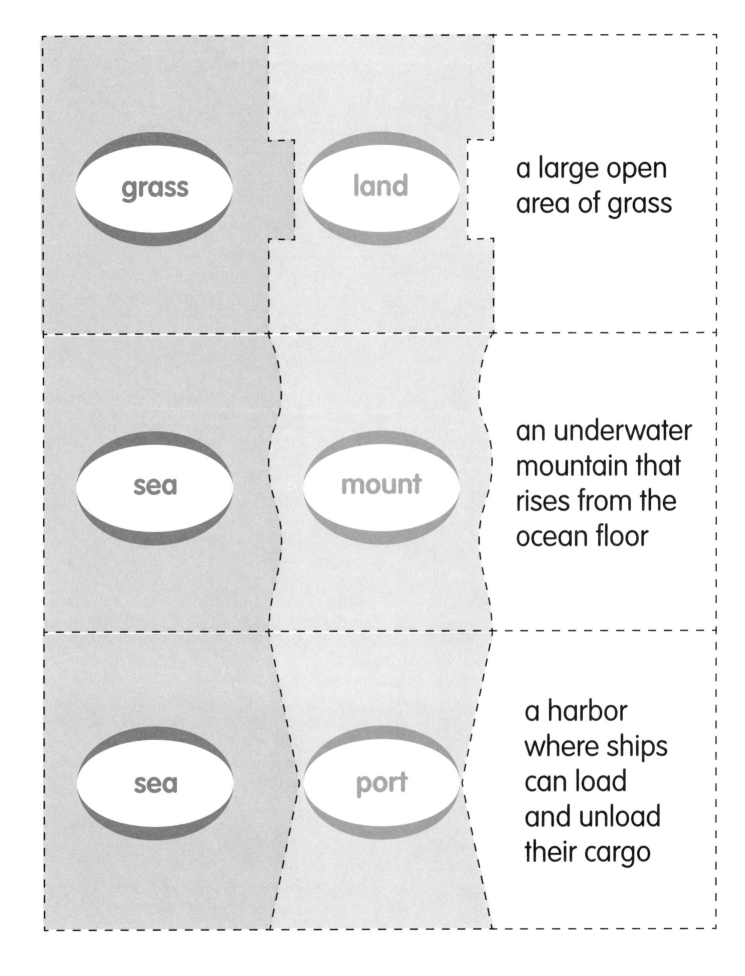

grass land · a large open area of grass

sea mount · an underwater mountain that rises from the ocean floor

sea port · a harbor where ships can load and unload their cargo

**Geography
Compound Words**

EMC 3350
© Evan-Moor Corp.

**Geography
Compound Words**

EMC 3350
© Evan-Moor Corp.

**Geography
Compound Words**

EMC 3350
© Evan-Moor Corp.

**Geography
Compound Words**

EMC 3350
© Evan-Moor Corp.

**Geography
Compound Words**

EMC 3350
© Evan-Moor Corp.

**Geography
Compound Words**

EMC 3350
© Evan-Moor Corp.

**Geography
Compound Words**

EMC 3350
© Evan-Moor Corp.

**Geography
Compound Words**

EMC 3350
© Evan-Moor Corp.

**Geography
Compound Words**

EMC 3350
© Evan-Moor Corp.

land

mass

a very large
area of land
such as
a continent

mountain

top

the highest
point on a
mountain

country

side

undeveloped
land away from
towns and cities

**Geography
Compound Words**

EMC 3350
© Evan-Moor Corp.

**Geography
Compound Words**

EMC 3350
© Evan-Moor Corp.

**Geography
Compound Words**

EMC 3350
© Evan-Moor Corp.

**Geography
Compound Words**

EMC 3350
© Evan-Moor Corp.

**Geography
Compound Words**

EMC 3350
© Evan-Moor Corp.

**Geography
Compound Words**

EMC 3350
© Evan-Moor Corp.

**Geography
Compound Words**

EMC 3350
© Evan-Moor Corp.

**Geography
Compound Words**

EMC 3350
© Evan-Moor Corp.

**Geography
Compound Words**

EMC 3350
© Evan-Moor Corp.

table

land

a high, broad, level area; another name for a plateau

water

front

any land or area of a city that is located by a body of water

whirl

pool

a current of water that moves quickly in a circle

**Geography
Compound Words**

EMC 3350
© Evan-Moor Corp.

**Geography
Compound Words**

EMC 3350
© Evan-Moor Corp.

**Geography
Compound Words**

EMC 3350
© Evan-Moor Corp.

**Geography
Compound Words**

EMC 3350
© Evan-Moor Corp.

**Geography
Compound Words**

EMC 3350
© Evan-Moor Corp.

**Geography
Compound Words**

EMC 3350
© Evan-Moor Corp.

**Geography
Compound Words**

EMC 3350
© Evan-Moor Corp.

**Geography
Compound Words**

EMC 3350
© Evan-Moor Corp.

**Geography
Compound Words**

EMC 3350
© Evan-Moor Corp.

Geography Compound Words

1. earthquake
2. everglade
3. downstream
4. seamount
5. grassland
6. seaport
7. landmass
8. countryside
9. mountaintop
10. waterfront
11. tableland
12. whirlpool

GEOGRAPHY COMPOUND WORDS

Lift the flap to check your answers.

Funny Nouns

Preparing the Center

1. Prepare a folder following the directions on page 3.

   Cover—page 117

   Student Directions—page 119

   Task Cards—pages 121–129

   Answer Key—page 131

2. Reproduce a supply of the activity sheet on page 116. Place copies in the left-hand pocket of the folder.

Partner Practice

1. The students sort the cards into three piles—funny nouns, definitions, and sentences.

2. Working together, the students match a funny noun with its definition and the sentence that uses the noun correctly. The cards are self-checking.

3. The students repeat Step 2 to match the other nine sets of cards. Encourage the students to take turns reading aloud the nouns, definitions, and sentences.

4. Then the students work cooperatively to complete their own activity sheet.

5. Finally, the students check their work using the answer key.

Independent Practice

1. The student sorts the cards into three piles—funny nouns, definitions, and sentences.

2. The student matches a funny noun to its definition and the sentence that uses the noun correctly. The cards are self-checking.

3. The student repeats Step 2 to match the other nine sets of cards. Encourage the student to read the cards aloud.

4. Then the student completes the activity sheet.

5. Finally, the student self-checks by using the answer key.

Funny Nouns

Find and circle the ten funny nouns. Words can go across, down, diagonally, or backward.

```
Z  G  H  D  Q  V  T  W  D  E  C  N  O  O
E  Z  F  U  I  L  I  I  G  R  H  O  K  Z
L  J  Z  O  M  N  D  D  L  Z  I  E  A  D
O  L  H  A  G  D  O  N  B  Q  T  G  B  K
D  K  E  D  T  P  I  G  I  Q  C  D  D  P
A  W  I  T  E  A  Z  N  D  W  H  U  B  O
F  N  P  G  I  L  M  D  G  O  A  M  N  P
G  R  D  A  Z  F  G  Z  A  E  T  R  K  V
U  O  K  U  O  G  F  Q  Z  D  R  U  I  B
H  L  O  H  N  L  Z  X  K  A  O  C  U  U
R  A  G  A  M  U  F  F  I  N  R  O  C  B
G  E  I  J  E  Y  W  N  W  M  N  A  D  B
Z  Q  G  I  W  G  I  B  Z  E  G  N  G  U
W  D  O  I  D  A  B  S  N  E  U  K  I  H
```

Word Box

bigwig	chitchat	curmudgeon
doodad	hodgepodge	hubbub
humdinger	ragamuffin	razzmatazz
wingding		

Funny Nouns

Word Wiz

A **noun** is a person, place, or thing.
Some nouns sound funny and old-fashioned.
They have been part of the English language for a long time.

Your great-grandmother might say this:
"I can't find that **doodad** anywhere."
A **doodad** is a small object whose name you can't think of.

Your great-grandfather might say this:
"You'd better go clean up, because you look like a **ragamuffin**."
A **ragamuffin** is a child who is dirty and ragged looking.

Follow These Steps

Partner Practice

1. Sort the cards into three piles—words, definitions, and sentences.

2. Match a funny noun with its definition and the sentence that uses the word correctly. Take turns reading the word, definition, and sentence aloud. Turn the cards over to check your work.

3. Repeat Step 2 to match the other nine sets of cards.

4. Work together to complete your own activity sheet.

5. Check your work using the answer key.

Independent Practice

1. Sort the cards into three piles—words, definitions, and sentences.

2. Match a funny noun with its definition and the sentence that uses the word correctly. Read the cards aloud. Turn the cards over to check your work.

3. Repeat Step 2 to match the other nine sets of cards.

4. Complete the activity sheet.

5. Check your work using the answer key.

bigwig  a person of great authority and importance

"People call me a _____ because I am the boss of a large company."

chitchat a light conversation; small talk

"It's fun having a _____ about what we are going to do at our next slumber party."

Funny Nouns

EMC 3350 • © Evan-Moor Corp.

Funny Nouns

EMC 3350 • © Evan-Moor Corp.

Funny Nouns

EMC 3350 • © Evan-Moor Corp.

Funny Nouns

EMC 3350 • © Evan-Moor Corp.

Funny Nouns

EMC 3350 • © Evan-Moor Corp.

Funny Nouns

EMC 3350 • © Evan-Moor Corp.

curmudgeon

a cranky person

"I don't think I am a _____ just because I won't let kids run through my yard."

doodad

a small object whose name you can't think of

"Grandma, what do you call this _____ that you use when you sew?"

Funny Nouns

EMC 3350 • © Evan-Moor Corp.

Funny Nouns

EMC 3350 • © Evan-Moor Corp.

Funny Nouns

EMC 3350 • © Evan-Moor Corp.

Funny Nouns

EMC 3350 • © Evan-Moor Corp.

Funny Nouns

EMC 3350 • © Evan-Moor Corp.

Funny Nouns

EMC 3350 • © Evan-Moor Corp.

hodgepodge

a jumbled
mixture
of things

"Let's just have a _____ of food
for dinner tonight."

hubbub

a mixture of
loud noises

"What's all the _____? I'm trying to sleep!"

Funny Nouns

EMC 3350 • © Evan-Moor Corp.

Funny Nouns

EMC 3350 • © Evan-Moor Corp.

Funny Nouns

EMC 3350 • © Evan-Moor Corp.

Funny Nouns

EMC 3350 • © Evan-Moor Corp.

Funny Nouns

EMC 3350 • © Evan-Moor Corp.

Funny Nouns

EMC 3350 • © Evan-Moor Corp.

humdinger

someone or something that is superior or very unusual

"Don't you think this fish I caught is a real _____?"

ragamuffin

a dirty, ragged-looking child

"I'd better take a shower before my mom calls me her little _____."

Funny Nouns

EMC 3350 • © Evan-Moor Corp.

Funny Nouns

EMC 3350 • © Evan-Moor Corp.

Funny Nouns

EMC 3350 • © Evan-Moor Corp.

Funny Nouns

EMC 3350 • © Evan-Moor Corp.

Funny Nouns

EMC 3350 • © Evan-Moor Corp.

Funny Nouns

EMC 3350 • © Evan-Moor Corp.

razzmatazz

a flashy display; showiness

"Ladies and gentlemen, this is what I call _____."

wingding

a lively event or party

"This is the best _____ I have ever been invited to."

Funny Nouns

EMC 3350 • © Evan-Moor Corp.

Funny Nouns

EMC 3350 • © Evan-Moor Corp.

Funny Nouns

EMC 3350 • © Evan-Moor Corp.

Funny Nouns

EMC 3350 • © Evan-Moor Corp.

Funny Nouns

EMC 3350 • © Evan-Moor Corp.

Funny Nouns

EMC 3350 • © Evan-Moor Corp.

Funny Nouns

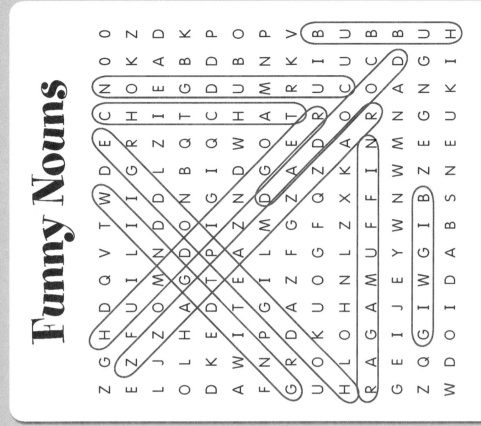

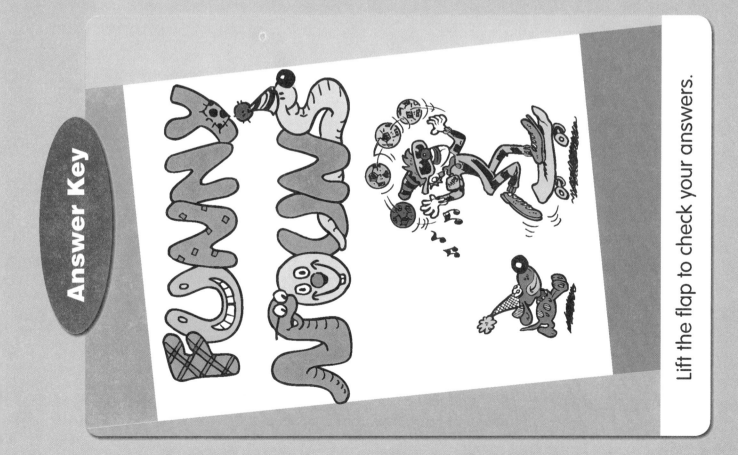

Lift the flap to check your answers.

Wild Weather Tic-Tac-Toe

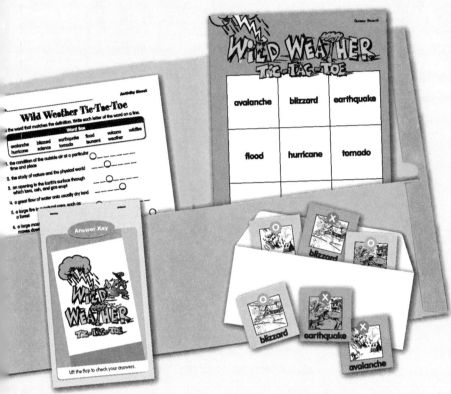

Preparing the Center

1. Prepare a folder following the directions on page 3.

    Cover—page 135

    Student Directions—page 137

    Game Rules—page 139

    Game Board—page 141

    Task Cards—pages 143 and 145

    Answer Key—page 147

2. Reproduce a supply of the activity sheet on page 134. Place copies in the left-hand pocket of the folder.

Partner Practice

1. The students read the tic-tac-toe rules for two players.

2. The students follow the rules to play the game. Encourage the students to read aloud the words and definitions. There are also kid-friendly pronunciations of the words on the backs of the cards.

3. Then the students work cooperatively to complete their own activity sheet.

4. Finally, the students check their work using the answer key.

Independent Practice

1. The student reads the tic-tac-toe rules for one player.

2. The student follows the rules to play the game. Remind the student to read aloud the front and back of each word card. Each card has the weather word and picture on the front and the definition and kid-friendly pronunciation on the back.

3. Then the student completes the activity sheet.

4. Finally, the student self-checks by using the answer key.

Name_____

Wild Weather Tic-Tac-Toe

Find the word that matches each definition. Write the words on the lines.

Word Box

avalanche	blizzard	earthquake	flood	volcano	wildfire
hurricane	science	tornado	tsunami	weather	

1. the condition of the outside air at a particular time and place

2. the study of nature and the physical world

3. an opening in the Earth's surface through which lava, ash, and gas erupt

4. a great flow of water onto usually dry land

5. a large fire in a natural area such as a forest

6. a large mass of snow, ice, or earth that moves down the side of a mountain

7. a huge funnel cloud that twists and swirls quickly over land

8. a very large and destructive wave of water

9. a sudden, violent shaking of the earth

10. a storm with heavy rain and strong winds that forms over the ocean

11. a heavy snowstorm with strong winds

Write the circled letters in order on the lines below to answer the riddle.

What part of the natural world should be tamed?

__ __ __ __ __ __ __ __ __ __ __

Take It to Your Seat—Vocabulary Centers • EMC 3350 • © Evan-Moor Corp.

Word Wiz

Special science words name and describe kinds of weather and natural disasters.

Tsunami is a special science word. It describes a kind of natural disaster.

A **tsunami** (tsoo-**nah**-mee) is a very large and destructive wave.

It is caused by an underwater earthquake or volcanic eruption.

Follow These Steps

Partner Practice

1. Take turns reading the tic-tac-toe rules for two players.

2. Play the game. Remember to read aloud the front and back of each card as you play the game.

3. Work together to complete your own activity sheet.

4. Check your work using the answer key.

Independent Practice

1. Read the tic-tac-toe rules for one player.

2. Play the game. Remember to read the front and back of each card aloud as you play the game.

3. Complete the activity sheet.

4. Check your work using the answer key.

Rules for 2 Players:

1. Choose which player will have the X word cards and which player will have the O word cards.

2. Take your cards and keep them in a pile, definition side up. Set the tic-tac-toe game board between the two of you.

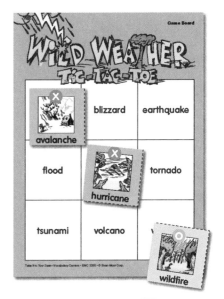

3. Let player X go first. The player reads aloud the first X word card and the definition. The player turns over the card and places it on the matching space on the game board.

4. Player O goes next. The player reads aloud the first O word card and its definition. The player turns over the card and places it on the matching space on the game board.

5. Take turns playing until one player has three symbols in a row. Or, play until the game board is filled, and no one has won.

6. Take turns having the X word cards.

Rules for 1 Player:

1. Shuffle the word cards and keep them in a pile, definition side up.

2. Pick the top card. Read aloud the word and its definition.

3. Turn the card over and place it on the corresponding space on the game board.

4. Continue playing until you have three X words or three O words in a row, or until you fill the game board.

avalanche	blizzard	earthquake
flood	hurricane	tornado
tsunami	volcano	wildfire

avalanche

blizzard

earthquake

flood

hurricane

tornado

tsunami

volcano

wildfire

earthquake
(**urth**-kwayk)

An **earthquake** is a sudden, violent shaking of the earth. An earthquake is caused by the shifting of the Earth's crust.

**Wild Weather
Tic-Tac-Toe**

EMC 3350 • © Evan-Moor Corp.

blizzard
(**bliz**-urd)

A **blizzard** is a heavy snowstorm with strong winds.

**Wild Weather
Tic-Tac-Toe**

EMC 3350 • © Evan-Moor Corp.

avalanche
(**av**-uh-lanch)

An **avalanche** is a large mass of snow, ice, or earth that suddenly moves down the side of a mountain.

**Wild Weather
Tic-Tac-Toe**

EMC 3350 • © Evan-Moor Corp.

tornado
(tor-**nay**-doh)

A **tornado** is a huge funnel cloud that twists and swirls very fast over land.

**Wild Weather
Tic-Tac-Toe**

EMC 3350 • © Evan-Moor Corp.

hurricane
(**hur**-uh-kane)

A **hurricane** is a powerful storm that forms over an ocean. A hurricane brings heavy rain and has strong, whirling winds.

**Wild Weather
Tic-Tac-Toe**

EMC 3350 • © Evan-Moor Corp.

flood
(fluhd)

A **flood** is a great flow of water onto land that usually is dry.

**Wild Weather
Tic-Tac-Toe**

EMC 3350 • © Evan-Moor Corp.

wildfire
(**wild**-fire)

A **wildfire** is a large fire in a natural area such as a forest.

**Wild Weather
Tic-Tac-Toe**

EMC 3350 • © Evan-Moor Corp.

volcano
(vol-**kay**-noh)

A **volcano** is an opening in the Earth's surface through which molten lava, ash, cinders, and gas erupt.

**Wild Weather
Tic-Tac-Toe**

EMC 3350 • © Evan-Moor Corp.

tsunami
(tsoo-**nah**-mee)

A **tsunami** is a very large and destructive wave caused by an underwater earthquake or volcanic eruption.

**Wild Weather
Tic-Tac-Toe**

EMC 3350 • © Evan-Moor Corp.

avalanche

blizzard

earthquake

flood

hurricane

tornado

tsunami

volcano

wildfire

earthquake
(urth-kwayk)

An **earthquake** is a sudden, violent shaking of the earth. An earthquake is caused by the shifting of the Earth's crust.

Wild Weather
Tic-Tac-Toe

EMC 3350 • © Evan-Moor Corp.

blizzard
(bliz-urd)

A **blizzard** is a heavy snowstorm with strong winds.

Wild Weather
Tic-Tac-Toe

EMC 3350 • © Evan-Moor Corp.

avalanche
(av-uh-lanch)

An **avalanche** is a large mass of snow, ice, or earth that suddenly moves down the side of a mountain.

Wild Weather
Tic-Tac-Toe

EMC 3350 • © Evan-Moor Corp.

tornado
(tor-**nay**-doh)

A **tornado** is a huge funnel cloud that twists and swirls very fast over land.

Wild Weather
Tic-Tac-Toe

EMC 3350 • © Evan-Moor Corp.

hurricane
(**hur**-uh-kane)

A **hurricane** is a powerful storm that forms over an ocean. A hurricane brings heavy rain and has strong, whirling winds.

Wild Weather
Tic-Tac-Toe

EMC 3350 • © Evan-Moor Corp.

flood
(fluhd)

A **flood** is a great flow of water onto land that usually is dry.

Wild Weather
Tic-Tac-Toe

EMC 3350 • © Evan-Moor Corp.

wildfire
(**wild**-fire)

A **wildfire** is a large fire in a natural area such as a forest.

Wild Weather
Tic-Tac-Toe

EMC 3350 • © Evan-Moor Corp.

volcano
(vol-**kay**-noh)

A **volcano** is an opening in the Earth's surface through which molten lava, ash, cinders, and gas erupt.

Wild Weather
Tic-Tac-Toe

EMC 3350 • © Evan-Moor Corp.

tsunami
(tsoo-**nah**-mee)

A **tsunami** is a very large and destructive wave caused by an underwater earthquake or volcanic eruption.

Wild Weather
Tic-Tac-Toe

EMC 3350 • © Evan-Moor Corp.

Wild Weather Tic-Tac-Toe

1. weather
2. science
3. volcano
4. flood
5. wildfire
6. avalanche
7. tornado
8. tsunami
9. earthquake
10. hurricane
11. blizzard

What part of the natural world should be tamed?

w i l d   w e a t h e r

Answer Key

Lift the flap to check your answers.

Playing with Polygons

Preparing the Center

1. Prepare a folder following the directions on page 3.

   Cover—page 151

   Student Directions—page 153

   Task Cards—pages 155–161

   Answer Key—page 163

2. Reproduce a supply of the activity sheet on page 150. Place copies in the left-hand pocket of the folder.

Partner Practice

1. Students sort the cards into four piles—words, definitions, pictures, and numbers.

2. Working together, the students match the name of the polygon with its picture, definition, and number of sides. The cards are self-checking.

3. The students repeat Step 2 to match the other seven sets of cards. Encourage the students to take turns reading the words and definitions aloud.

4. Then the students work cooperatively to complete their own activity sheet.

5. Finally, the students check their work using the answer key.

Independent Practice

1. The student sorts the cards into four piles—words, definitions, pictures, and numbers.

2. The student matches the name of the polygon with its picture, definition, and number of sides. The cards are self-checking.

3. The student repeats Step 2 to match the other seven sets of cards. Encourage the student to read the words and definitions aloud.

4. Then the student completes the activity sheet.

5. Finally, the student self-checks by using the answer key.

Playing with Polygons

Write the name of each polygon next to its picture. Use the word box to help you.

Word Box			
decagon	heptagon	hexagon	nonagon
octagon	pentagon	square	triangle

1. _____

2. _____

3. _____

4. _____

5. _____

6. _____

7. _____

8. _____

PLAYING WITH POLYGONS

Playing with Polygons

Student Directions

Word Wiz

Polygon is an important math term to know.
A polygon is a flat closed figure with three or more straight sides.

There are many kinds of polygons. Here are two examples:

A **triangle** is a polygon.
A triangle is a closed figure
with three straight sides.

A **pentagon** is a polygon.
A pentagon is a closed
figure with five straight sides.

Follow These Steps

Partner Practice

1. Sort the cards into four piles—words, pictures, definitions, and numbers.

2. Match a polygon name with its picture, definition, and number of sides. Take turns reading aloud the polygon name and its definition. Turn the set of four cards over to check your work.

3. Repeat Step 2 to match the other seven sets of cards.

4. Work together to complete your own activity sheet.

5. Check your work using the answer key.

Independent Practice

1. Sort the cards into four piles—words, pictures, definitions, and numbers.

2. Match a polygon name with its picture, definition, and number of sides. Read aloud the polygon name and its definition. Turn the set of four cards over to check your work.

3. Repeat Step 2 to match the other seven sets of cards.

4. Complete the activity sheet.

5. Check your work using the answer key.

154

decagon

a polygon that has ten sides

10

heptagon

a polygon that
has seven sides

7

Playing with Polygons

EMC 3350 • © Evan-Moor Corp.

Playing with Polygons

EMC 3350 • © Evan-Moor Corp.

Playing with Polygons

EMC 3350 • © Evan-Moor Corp.

Playing with Polygons

EMC 3350 • © Evan-Moor Corp.

Playing with Polygons

EMC 3350 • © Evan-Moor Corp.

Playing with Polygons

EMC 3350 • © Evan-Moor Corp..

Playing with Polygons

EMC 3350 • © Evan-Moor Corp..

Playing with Polygons

EMC 3350 • © Evan-Moor Corp.

hexagon

6

a polygon that has six sides

nonagon

9

a polygon that has nine sides

Playing with Polygons

EMC 3350 • © Evan-Moor Corp.

Playing with Polygons

EMC 3350 • © Evan-Moor Corp.

Playing with Polygons

EMC 3350 • © Evan-Moor Corp.

Playing with Polygons

EMC 3350 • © Evan-Moor Corp.

Playing with Polygons

EMC 3350 • © Evan-Moor Corp.

Playing with Polygons

EMC 3350 • © Evan-Moor Corp.

Playing with Polygons

EMC 3350 • © Evan-Moor Corp.

Playing with Polygons

EMC 3350 • © Evan-Moor Corp.

octagon

8

a polygon that
has eight sides

pentagon

5

a polygon that has five sides

Playing with Polygons

EMC 3350 • © Evan-Moor Corp.

Playing with Polygons

EMC 3350 • © Evan-Moor Corp.

Playing with Polygons

EMC 3350 • © Evan-Moor Corp.

Playing with Polygons

EMC 3350 • © Evan-Moor Corp.

Playing with Polygons

EMC 3350 • © Evan-Moor Corp.

Playing with Polygons

EMC 3350 • © Evan-Moor Corp.

Playing with Polygons

EMC 3350 • © Evan-Moor Corp.

Playing with Polygons

EMC 3350 • © Evan-Moor Corp.

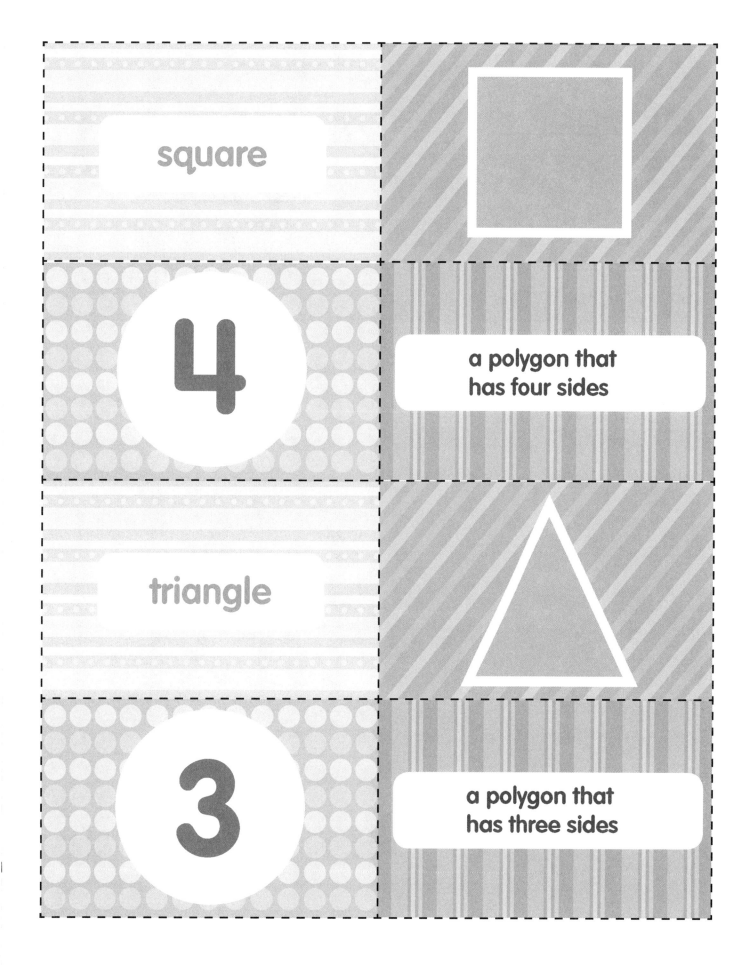

square

4

a polygon that
has four sides

triangle

a polygon that
has three sides

3

Playing with Polygons

EMC 3350 • © Evan-Moor Corp.

Playing with Polygons

EMC 3350 • © Evan-Moor Corp.

Playing with Polygons

EMC 3350 • © Evan-Moor Corp.

Playing with Polygons

EMC 3350 • © Evan-Moor Corp..

Playing with Polygons

EMC 3350 • © Evan-Moor Corp.

Playing with Polygons

EMC 3350 • © Evan-Moor Corp.

Playing with Polygons

EMC 3350 • © Evan-Moor Corp.

Playing with Polygons

EMC 3350 • © Evan-Moor Corp.

Playing with Polygons

1. triangle

2. heptagon

3. square

4. hexagon

5. octagon

6. pentagon

7. nonagon

8. decagon

PLAYING WITH POLYGONS

Lift the flap to check your answers.

Borrowed Words

Preparing the Center

1. Prepare a folder following the directions on page 3.

   Cover—page 167

   Student Directions—page 169

   Puzzle Pieces—pages 171–175

   Answer Key—page 177

2. Reproduce a supply of the activity sheet on page 166. Place copies in the left-hand pocket of the folder.

Partner Practice

1. The students sort the puzzle pieces into two piles—definitions and words that have been borrowed from the Spanish language.

2. Working together, the students fit a word to its definition to form a two-part puzzle.

3. The students repeat Step 2 to complete the other 11 puzzles. Encourage the students to take turns as they read the words and definitions aloud.

4. Then the students work cooperatively to complete their own activity sheet.

5. Finally, the students check their work using the answer key.

Independent Practice

1. The student sorts the puzzle pieces into two piles—definitions and words that have been borrowed from the Spanish language.

2. The student fits a word to its definition to form a two-part puzzle.

3. The student repeats Step 2 to complete the other 11 puzzles. Encourage the student to read the words and definitions aloud.

4. Then the student completes the activity sheet.

5. Finally, the student self-checks by using the answer key.

Borrowed Words

Complete each sentence with the correct word from the box.

Word Box					
bronco	buckaroo	chaps	corral	lasso	mesa
mustangs	palomino	pinto	ranch	rodeo	stampede

1. The cowgirl used her _____ to catch the runaway steer.

2. The _____ competition included riding and roping skills.

3. A _____ happened because the herd of cattle was frightened.

4. In the Old West, a cowboy was sometimes called a _____.

5. The bucking _____ tossed the cowboy onto the ground.

6. I put _____ on my legs before I go horseback riding.

7. Wild _____ roam the prairies of the western United States.

8. From the top of the _____, the lone cowboy could see for miles.

9. The young girl wants that _____ pony because she likes the brown and white patches on his back.

10. The rancher fixed the _____ so the horses could not escape again.

11. The cowboy brushed the white mane of his golden _____.

12. A _____ is very large because it takes many acres of grassland to feed a herd of cattle.

Borrowed Words

Borrowed Words

Word Wiz

Many American English words dealing with the Wild West and cowboys are borrowed from Spanish words. That's because American cowboys worked with Mexican cowboys called **vaqueros** (vah-**kair**-ohz).

The word **bronco** means "wild or rough" in Spanish.
In American English, the word **bronco** refers to a wild horse.

In Spanish, **rancho** means "a settlement or camp."
In American English, the word **rancho** became **ranch**.

Follow These Steps

Partner Practice

1. Sort the puzzle pieces into two piles—words and definitions.

2. Working together, fit a word to its definition to complete the puzzle.

3. Repeat Step 2 to complete the other 11 puzzles. Take turns reading the words and definitions aloud.

4. Work together to complete your own activity sheet.

5. Check your work using the answer key.

Independent Practice

1. Sort the puzzle pieces into two piles—words and definitions.

2. Fit a word to its definition to complete the puzzle.

3. Repeat Step 2 to complete the other 11 puzzles. Read the words and definitions aloud.

4. Complete the activity sheet.

5. Check your work using the answer key.

bronco
(**brong**-ko)

a wild, untamed horse found in the western United States that is often used for rodeo riding

buckaroo
(**buhk**-ah-roo)

another name for a cowboy

chaps
(chaps)

leather leggings that fit over pants and protect the legs of people riding on horseback

corral
(kuh-**ral**)

a fenced area that holds horses, cattle, or other animals

Borrowed Words

EMC 3350 • © Evan-Moor Corp.

Borrowed Words

EMC 3350 • © Evan-Moor Corp.

Borrowed Words

EMC 3350 • © Evan-Moor Corp.

Borrowed Words

EMC 3350 • © Evan-Moor Corp.

Borrowed Words

EMC 3350 • © Evan-Moor Corp.

Borrowed Words

EMC 3350 • © Evan-Moor Corp.

Borrowed Words

EMC 3350 • © Evan-Moor Corp.

Borrowed Words

EMC 3350 • © Evan-Moor Corp.

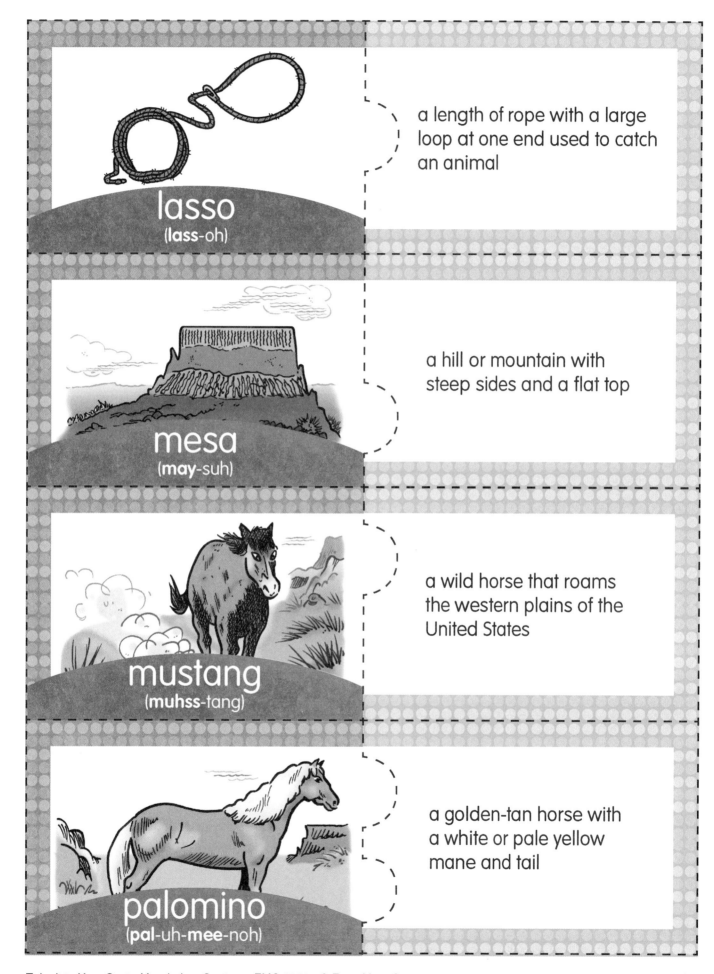

lasso
(**lass**-oh)

a length of rope with a large loop at one end used to catch an animal

mesa
(**may**-suh)

a hill or mountain with steep sides and a flat top

mustang
(**muhss**-tang)

a wild horse that roams the western plains of the United States

palomino
(**pal**-uh-**mee**-noh)

a golden-tan horse with a white or pale yellow mane and tail

Borrowed Words
EMC 3350 • © Evan-Moor Corp.

Borrowed Words
EMC 3350 • © Evan-Moor Corp.

Borrowed Words
EMC 3350 • © Evan-Moor Corp.

Borrowed Words
EMC 3350 • © Evan-Moor Corp.

Borrowed Words
EMC 3350 • © Evan-Moor Corp.

Borrowed Words
EMC 3350 • © Evan-Moor Corp.

Borrowed Words
EMC 3350 • © Evan-Moor Corp.

Borrowed Words
EMC 3350 • © Evan-Moor Corp.

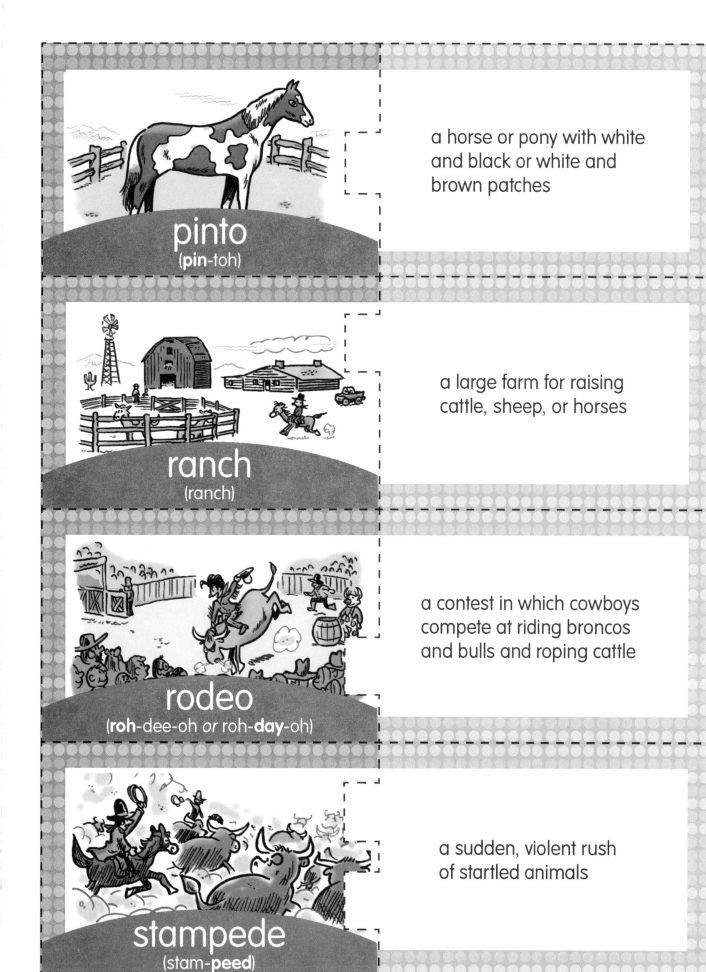

pinto
(**pin**-toh)

a horse or pony with white and black or white and brown patches

ranch
(ranch)

a large farm for raising cattle, sheep, or horses

rodeo
(**roh**-dee-oh *or* roh-**day**-oh)

a contest in which cowboys compete at riding broncos and bulls and roping cattle

stampede
(stam-**peed**)

a sudden, violent rush of startled animals

Borrowed Words

EMC 3350 • © Evan-Moor Corp.

Borrowed Words

EMC 3350 • © Evan-Moor Corp.

Borrowed Words

EMC 3350 • © Evan-Moor Corp.

Borrowed Words

EMC 3350 • © Evan-Moor Corp.

Borrowed Words

EMC 3350 • © Evan-Moor Corp.

Borrowed Words

EMC 3350 • © Evan-Moor Corp.

Borrowed Words

EMC 3350 • © Evan-Moor Corp.

Borrowed Words

EMC 3350 • © Evan-Moor Corp.

Borrowed Words

1. lasso
2. rodeo
3. stampede
4. buckaroo
5. bronco
6. chaps

7. mustangs
8. mesa
9. pinto
10. corral
11. palomino
12. ranch

Borrowed Words

Lift the flap to check your answers.

Multiple Meanings

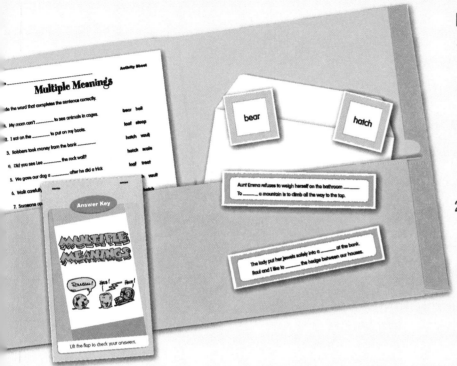

Preparing the Center

1. Prepare a folder following the directions on page 3.

   Cover—page 181

   Student Directions—page 183

   Task Cards—pages 185–189

   Answer Key—page 191

2. Reproduce a supply of the activity sheet on page 180. Place copies in the left-hand pocket of the folder.

Partner Practice

1. The students sort the cards into two piles—sentences and multiple-meaning words.

2. Working together, the students read each pair of sentences aloud. They find the word that correctly completes both sentences. The students turn over each set of cards to check their work.

3. Then the students work cooperatively to complete their own activity sheet.

4. Finally, the students check their work using the answer key.

Independent Practice

1. The student sorts the cards into two piles—sentences and multiple-meaning words.

2. The student reads aloud each pair of sentences. The student finds the word that correctly completes both sentences. The student turns over each set of cards to check the answer.

3. Then the student completes the activity sheet.

4. Finally, the student self-checks by using the answer key.

Multiple Meanings

Circle the word that correctly completes each sentence.

1. My mom can't _____ to see animals in cages. **bear**   **hail**

2. I sat on the _____ to put on my boots. **loaf**   **stoop**

3. Robbers took money from the bank _____. **hatch**   **vault**

4. Did you see Lee _____ the rock wall? **hatch**   **scale**

5. We gave our dog a _____ after he did a trick. **loaf**   **treat**

6. Walk carefully so you don't _____ any beetles. **squash**   **vault**

7. Someone opened the _____ so I could escape to safety. **hail**   **hatch**

8. Auntie Lisa uses chili powder to _____ her stew. **pound**   **season**

9. Please buy a _____ of hamburger at the grocery store. **loaf**   **pound**

10. I want to _____ in front of the TV for a while. **loaf**   **stoop**

11. Do you think the clouds will _____ our plans for a picnic? **hamper**   **scale**

12. The _____ fell from the sky and covered the ground. **bear**   **hail**

Multiple Meanings

Word Wiz

Multiple-meaning words are two or more words that have the same spelling but different meanings.

In this center, the multiple-meaning words are pairs of words that are used as both a noun and a verb.

noun
The **float** for the parade was made of colorful flowers.

verb
We will **float** gently down the river in a canoe.

Follow These Steps

Partner Practice

1. Sort the cards into two piles— sentences and words.

2. Working together, read aloud the two sentences on a card. Find the multiple-meaning word that correctly completes both sentences. Turn the two cards over to check your work.

3. Repeat Step 2 to match the other 11 words and sentences.

4. Work together to complete your own activity sheet.

5. Check your work using the answer key.

Independent Practice

1. Sort the cards into two piles— sentences and words.

2. Read aloud the two sentences on a card. Find the multiple-meaning word that correctly completes both sentences. Turn the two cards over to check your work.

3. Repeat Step 2 to match the other 11 words and sentences.

4. Complete the activity sheet.

5. Check your work using the answer key.

The grizzly _____ caught a salmon in the river.

Grandma can't _____ to see little children cry.

The storm produced icy balls of _____.

Tell Dad to _____ us a taxi so we can go to the hotel.

Mom asked me to put my dirty clothes in the _____.

I hope that the rain doesn't _____ our plans to go camping.

The sailor opened the _____ so he could go below deck.

We hope the chicks will _____ from the eggs soon.

I am so hungry that I could eat a whole _____ of bread.

Samantha likes to _____ around the house and not do any work.

Kevin went to the store to buy a _____ of butter and a gallon of milk.

My brother Victor likes to _____ nails into boards.

Multiple Meanings

EMC 3350 • © Evan-Moor Corp.

Multiple Meanings

EMC 3350 • © Evan-Moor Corp.

Multiple Meanings

EMC 3350 • © Evan-Moor Corp.

Multiple Meanings

EMC 3350 • © Evan-Moor Corp.

Multiple Meanings

EMC 3350 • © Evan-Moor Corp.

Multiple Meanings

EMC 3350 • © Evan-Moor Corp.

Aunt Emma refuses to weigh herself on the bathroom _____.

To _____ a mountain is to climb all the way to the top.

My favorite _____ of the year is summer.

Uncle Max likes to _____ his famous stew with salt and pepper.

It's time to pick the pumpkins and _____ from the garden.

Be careful where you are walking so you don't _____ any bugs.

Sit down on the _____ so you can take off your muddy shoes.

Ben had to _____ over to pick up the book he had dropped.

The teacher gives us a special _____ if we do our homework.

It is important to _____ animals with kindness.

The lady put her jewels safely into a _____ at the bank.

Raul and I like to _____ the hedge between our houses.

Multiple Meanings

EMC 3350 • © Evan-Moor Corp.

Multiple Meanings

EMC 3350 • © Evan-Moor Corp.

Multiple Meanings

EMC 3350 • © Evan-Moor Corp.

Multiple Meanings

EMC 3350 • © Evan-Moor Corp.

Multiple Meanings

EMC 3350 • © Evan-Moor Corp.

Multiple Meanings

EMC 3350 • © Evan-Moor Corp.

bear	hail	hamper
hatch	loaf	pound
scale	season	squash
stoop	treat	vault

Multiple Meanings

EMC 3350 • © Evan-Moor Corp.

Multiple Meanings

EMC 3350 • © Evan-Moor Corp.

Multiple Meanings

EMC 3350 • © Evan-Moor Corp.

Multiple Meanings

EMC 3350 • © Evan-Moor Corp.

Multiple Meanings

EMC 3350 • © Evan-Moor Corp.

Multiple Meanings

EMC 3350 • © Evan-Moor Corp.

Multiple Meanings

EMC 3350 • © Evan-Moor Corp.

Multiple Meanings

EMC 3350 • © Evan-Moor Corp.

Multiple Meanings

EMC 3350 • © Evan-Moor Corp.

Multiple Meanings

EMC 3350 • © Evan-Moor Corp.

Multiple Meanings

EMC 3350 • © Evan-Moor Corp.

Multiple Meanings

EMC 3350 • © Evan-Moor Corp.

Multiple Meanings

1. bear
2. stoop
3. vault
4. scale
5. treat
6. squash

7. hatch
8. season
9. pound
10. loaf
11. hamper
12. hail

MULTIPLE MEANINGS

HERE!

HERE!

ROLLCALL!

TAPE

Lift the flap to check your answers.

192